The Perfect Teacher

Also available from Continuum

Managing Very Challenging Behaviour, Louisa Leaman

Classroom Confidential, Louisa Leaman

The Naked Teacher, Louisa Leaman

The Dictionary of Disruption, Louisa Leaman

Guerilla Guide to Teaching, Sue Cowley

The Ultimate Teachers' Handbook, Hazel Bennett

The Perfect Teacher

How to make the very best of your teaching skills

Louisa Leaman

continuum

Continuum International Publishing Group
The Tower Building   80 Maiden Lane
11 York Road   Suite 704
London   New York
SE1 7NX   NY 10038

www.continuumbooks.com

British Library Cataloguing-in-Publication Data
A catalogue record for this book is available from the British Library.

ISBN: 9780826497871 (paperback)

Library of Congress Cataloging-in-Publication Data
Louisa, Leaman.
The perfect teacher: how to make the very best of your teaching skills/Louisa Leaman.
    p. cm.
Includes index.
ISBN: 978-0-8264-9787-1
1. Effective teaching. 2. Classroom management. I. Title.

LB1025.3.L4165 2008
371.102--dc22   2008017834

Typeset by Newgen Imaging Systems Pvt Ltd, Chennai, India
Printed and bound in Great Britain by Cromwell Press, Wiltshire

Contents

Acknowledgements

With special thanks to Julian, Mike, Sheila, Ray, Diane, Sue, Pete, Graham, Cheryl, Jude, and Thom. And to everyone else who contributed their thoughts and experiences along the way. Also thanks to Anthony Haynes and everyone at Continuum.

Introduction

Whenever I mention the title of this book to teaching friends and colleagues, the reaction I get is pretty much standard: a slow rolling back of the eyes, a scornful shaking of the head, and some kind of dry comment along the lines of: 'Perfect teachers? Hah! Yea right! No such thing!' But they are right to be suspicious. The idea of perfection is a difficult one to quantify, and in a profession such as teaching, where there are so many variables (let alone challenges), summing up the specific credentials for perfection is near impossible.

Therefore, throughout this book, you will find that the term 'perfect' is used with a pinch of salt. My intention is not to squeeze everyone into uniform-sized boxes, each labelled 'perfect'; but it is to help teachers, at any stage of their career, to find their own idea of perfection (or at least success) within their own teaching environment.

'The Perfect Teacher' is a practical guide that lights up the shadows of the classroom by providing a multi-faceted insight into what works. Acting as a critical friend, it helps you to reflect on your own skills and strengths, whilst offering a range of viewpoints that may throw up new and fresh solutions to old problems. The guide explores major issues of the profession, such as behaviour management, teaching and learning, coping with stressful situations, and building positive relationships with pupils and staff.

I have taken the perspectives of different education-related professionals as a starting point. Many of the thoughts and suggestions were generated through discussion groups, which brought together a varied cross-section of individuals. I have collaborated with colleagues up and down the country, including classroom teachers (primary and secondary), newly qualified teachers (NQTs), special needs teachers, head teachers, deputy head teachers, social workers, special education needs coordinators (SENCOs), teaching assistants, lecturers, educational psychologists, Office for Standards in Education (OFSTED) inspectors and school governors; and also, importantly, parents and pupils. This has ensured that the information in these pages is representative of many different opinions, providing a broad and balanced profile of 'perfection' – and a truthful one.

All of the individuals that I have consulted with have had their own tales to tell and their own set of experiences to share. It has been fascinating, encouraging, reassuring and sometimes eye-opening; but above all, it has made me realise just how much knowledge is actually out there – knowledge that comes from genuine, hands-on experience. We all know that this sort of knowledge is invaluable, so I like to think that 'The Perfect Teacher' is bringing much of it together and making it accessible.

So what can The 'Perfect' Teacher do for you?

Perhaps you've been doing teaching for years – you know the ropes by now. You don't need some stuck-up, out-of-touch, hasn't-been-in-a-classroom-since-1968, interfering old busybody telling you that whole-class detentions are a violation of the human rights act. Or perhaps you've just started out. You're an NQT– but hey, you were the only person in your college to get a Teaching and Learning Responsibility point before you completed your training year; and over the summer, you read *every* behaviour management book on the shelf. In two years time, you'll be running this place. What can other peoples' opinions do for you?

For those who are able to keep their eyes open and their egos on the ground, teaching is a profession in which the teachers themselves are continuously learning. There is never a shortage of different challenges to tackle, or new personalities to contend with, because there is a never-ending flow of new pupils and new initiatives.

My own mother (a retired English teacher), when trying to herd me towards what she thought was a 'sensible' career, made the point that at least teaching never gets dull. I discovered how right she was the moment I entered my first classroom of pupils as an innocent NQT. If it wasn't the cheeky remarks, it was the ridiculous questions, and if it wasn't the questions, it was the bizarre interpretations of homework, and if it wasn't the homework, it was the incessant probing into my private life. I couldn't stop for a second, and I couldn't take my eye of the ball; but I found myself enjoying the challenge.

I did, however, discover that there is, in fact, a very boring side to teaching, one that my mother cautiously kept quiet about, and that is *the paperwork*. And when the paperwork just kept coming, I realised that successful teaching demands a lot more than simply being able to hold up your end in a bit of classroom banter. It requires 'organisational skills' – a phrase that used to make me feel woefully inadequate. Over the years, I paid attention to what the really efficient teachers were doing and managed to get my act together. And along the way, I noticed how improvements in planning and general organisation also improved my lessons. I realised that one skill can support another. I also realised that I, alone, didn't have all the answers.

Although schools are busy places, spending most of your day in the company of 30+ children can feel rather lonely. There is precious little time for teachers to make meaningful contact with other staff members. A quick catch-up in the car park, or a bit of off-loading in the staff-room – such things can work wonders for frazzled colleagues; but chances to really talk about what happens in our classrooms, and to share our ideas, can easily be overtaken by all the other jobs that need doing. And when these opportunities do arise, they are often in formal circumstances: inspections, observations, appraisals and training days.

As a result, it can sometimes be difficult for people to develop a fair view of their own practice. Many teachers are overly self-critical, because they rarely get to see that they are not the only ones who struggle with certain students or have difficulties keeping up with the workload. Some find it tough, because they become too insular – they get stuck in the same routines, or feel that they have run out of ideas. Others become demoralised – they feel over criticised, undervalued and very misunderstood.

For the amount of times I have heard delegates on my training days say: "It's so nice to get the chance to talk to other teachers", or "It's made me realise that I'm not the only one who has difficulties!" I sometimes wonder whether teachers talk to each other at all! But isolation is just one part of it. We've all heard (or made) gripes about the head teachers and OFSTED inspectors who are rarely seen taking responsibility for teaching a class, yet are quick to judge the actions of those who do. What do *they* know? They just sit in their offices twiddling their thumbs and scribbling out numbers on budget sheets. Don't they?

Then, of course, there are the parents: the ones who know best. The ones who never seem satisfied that their son/daughter is being treated fairly or given enough one-to-one attention. Or the ones who are never available, who are never at the end of one of their many mobile phone lines, despite the fact that their child has climbed on the gym roof and is now hurling abuse at innocent passers by.

And what about the pupils? Who will inevitably have something to say about your classroom methods: 'You're too bossy.' 'Your lessons are too easy.' 'You're always telling *me* off, but what about him?' 'You aren't as good as our last teacher. . .' Effectively, they are the ones who are on the receiving end, so it stands to reason that we should take time to listen, analyse and reflect on what they have to say about their experience of education. But do we really want to when something tells us they're just trying to wind us up?

And, of course, you cannot forget your colleagues: the other teachers and school staff. Many wonderful, lovely supportive ones, but there are always one or two who will feel obliged to kick you further down the ladder of life by pointing out that so-and-so never behaves like that in *their* lessons. Well bully for them! At least you don't have to resort to undermining others, in order to aggrandise yourself.

It seems that everyone has an opinion about teaching. You only need to turn on the evening news to hear that there is some new initiative, scandal or problem that has just been uncovered in our schools. This continuous interfering, judging and scrutinising of our practice – from all corners of society, from government inspectors to mouthy students – can be draining and demoralising. That's not to say that it cannot also, at times, be useful; in that it can help to challenge, refresh and raise standards.

Perhaps something teachers would appreciate is the knowledge that the people who are passing judgement on what goes on in their classrooms actually have a genuine understanding of what it is to do that job and what challenges teachers face. It is about seeing the bigger picture – not just viewing each problem in isolation, but from within in the context of the whole system. As teachers, we have to balance many different expectations and responsibilities during our school day – it can often feel like an impossible task, and this has nothing to do with the quality of our teaching. I, for one, would like to see some of the people who complain about failing teachers, stand up and try it for themselves!

Because of these different strains, I decided I needed to write a book that would bring together the opinions and ideas, not just of teachers (although they provide a valuable backbone of information), but of different individuals involved in education: from the 'service user', to the 'service manager'. I hope you find it as interesting and helpful to read and reflect upon, as I have researching it.

Of course, I can't guarantee that reading it will turn you into a perfect teacher – that's down to you and your particular circumstances. But hopefully it will encourage you to feel confident about your practice, inspired to try new things, and feel reassured that you are not alone when it doesn't go the way you want it to. Good luck.

1 You and your teaching style

Teacher personality

One of the principal themes that emerged, whilst researching 'The Perfect Teacher' is that there is no 'one-size-fits-all' magic answer to what happens in the classroom. The perfect teacher is perhaps better phrased as perfect *teachers*, for it seems that professional success is determined by a broad number of variables, such as the type of school, type of pupils, type of teacher expectations, type of lesson/subject being taught. What makes someone thrive in one situation may cause problems in another. For example, staff that were working in some of the more 'academic' schools that I consulted felt that their rigorous and formal approach to classwork would be buried by the demands of challenging students within a school where behavioural problems were a primary concern. Likewise, there were teachers who professed to being more motivated by building meaningful relationships with some of the more difficult students, focusing on self-esteem and personality, rather than academic results.

Nowhere is the need to consider the benefits of variety more prevalent, than when we come to consider 'teacher personality'. By this, I mean the persona that we create for ourselves in front of our students. Inevitably this persona is wrapped up with our more general personality traits, for instance, whether we may be outgoing or shy or quick-humoured or bossy. But there are always those that we might least expect: the quiet, mouse-like Spanish teacher, who hides in the corner of the staff-room and doesn't speak – turns out all the students are terrified of her!

Many of the teachers I consulted, talked about their classroom practice as a kind of performance, or act. Indeed, they also suggested that this is a helpful thing. It enables them to feel strong in front of the students, to project an air of confidence and authority, even when they are feeling less than sure of themselves. One experienced teacher suggested:

> It's about distance. If you give away too much of your true self, you become vulnerable and risk having your authority undermined. You can give away little hints, to remind them that you are human, but if you do it too much they will use it to their advantage. Generally, you have to appear like you are in complete command, and just step into that role each time you enter the classroom – but it's difficult to maintain all of the time.

She also offered some reassurance:

> Everyone has their off days. I think it gets easier as you become more experienced. When you first start teaching, you are much more aware of it being an act, but eventually you get used to the role and it becomes second-nature – the hardest thing is switching it off when you get home again!

Reflection box:
How easily do you slip into your teaching 'role'? Are you unaware of it, or do you sometimes wish you had more time to rehearse? Do you find yourself playing different characters in front of different classes?

Whether acting or not, the kind of teacher personality traits that people felt were most effective in the classroom were the following:

Having a sense of humour
Being upbeat
Being caring (but slightly removed)
Focusing on respect (not popularity)
Being firm with the rules, friendly with individuals.

Humour repeatedly emerged as a valuable trait, not just from the teacher's perspective, but from the pupil's point of view too.

Many of those I consulted referred fondly to the type of teacher who made them all laugh. Used judiciously, humour has many benefits, ranging from bringing an otherwise dull subject matter to life; to diffusing a potential conflict. But, of course, it is a method that carries many risks, including the possibility of not quite pulling it off. Can you get away with pretending to be funny, even if it doesn't come naturally? One secondary school pupil cautioned:

> It annoys me when teachers, particularly the young ones, try too hard to impress and to be funny. If they aren't being natural, everyone can tell, and it usually means they will be given a hard time.

When asked if he thought this was fair, the pupil replied:

> I think teachers should just be themselves. As long as they aren't rude or always moaning, then we don't mind. We don't like fake people.

So if you're worried they might see through the ropey stand-up comic routine, are there other ways of making your lessons entertaining and is it really necessary? An experienced secondary teacher suggested that bringing energy, fun and humour to the classroom is vital, but does not have to be too daunting:

> The curriculum can sometimes be tediously prescriptive, dull and 'bitty'. So a good teacher should be able to take a boring piece of work, and by use of voice and personality and the way they introduce it, bring it to life and make it exciting. For example, when I do sentence work, I use daft phrases that take the pupils by surprise, which helps to make it memorable. It's not a lot of effort on my part. It just requires a bit of imagination.

The desire to enliven the curriculum is consistently echoed by teachers and pupils alike. It seems that many are searching for their own inspirational 'Mr Chips' character, who is perhaps the archetypal 'perfect' teacher. Refreshingly, it seems that only one or two memorable lessons are what it takes to make an initial impact. Do something that grabs their attention every now and again (you may find some ideas in this book), and even if the majority of your lessons are more 'formal', they will be hanging on tenterhooks waiting to see what's coming next. You might just be the one that makes the difference. A successful poet, reflecting on her own experience at primary school, explained:

> I had one teacher that was amazingly inspiring. She once used my own poem in an exam, without telling me. It took me a moment to realise it was mine. When I did, I asked her why she'd used it – she just shrugged and said it deserved to be noticed. That moment made me feel really special and inspired me to keep writing poetry.

Reflection box:
What is the most bold, daring thing you've done to get pupils interested in you and your lessons? And what, if anything, puts you off trying different things?

Teachers were unified when it came to considering the personality traits that are least effective. These are the definite no-nos:

Being dull and un-engaging
Obvious disinterest in the work
Being uncaring
Not making an effort
Inconsistency
Bullying
Egos getting in the way
Power-trips
Nasty sarcasm

Much discussions were had over the theme of lack of effort and passion for the work. Several teachers argued that that this is not so much about having a teaching style that lacks sparkle and effervescence, but about not caring, or committing to the responsibilities of the role. In other words, the biggest crime is not being an un-dynamic teacher, but being a lazy one. A primary head teacher highlighted the statement: *education should be about setting things on fire, not filling buckets*. He then went onto articulate what he looked for in potential teaching candidates:

> Individuals who project a personality that is not powerful and overbearing, but lively, empathetic, sympathetic and 'brave'. Their confidence has got to come across, but it's a special kind of confidence. It's about caring. I want my staff to have a commitment to giving, and getting, the best from the job.

I asked teachers what they thought of the good old cliché: 'Don't smile till Christmas'. The common reaction was an accepting nod, although some made the concession that Christmas was probably too long to wait. Several individuals said that the phrase helped remind them that teachers are never the kids' friends – it's a professional relationship, and this needs to be established right from the start. However, this isn't always easy, as one recently qualified teacher suggested:

> I tried the 'don't smile till Christmas' thing with my tutor group in my first year, but after two days I cracked, because they were so funny and friendly . . . the job is more enjoyable if I can interact with my pupils in the way I'm used to. I did have difficulties with them, and had to work quite hard to keep them in line, but ultimately, it wasn't my personality to be all stern and grumpy. And actually, at the end of the day, they enjoyed my company and I enjoyed theirs.

And you don't hear that very often!

Key points for teacher personality:
> ➤ Play to your personality strengths, but be prepared to adapt your style according to the age, attitude and ability of your pupils.
> ➤ Think of it as an act, a professional role, and reassure yourself that everyone feels like a fraud at times.
> ➤ Be careful about how much of your personal self you reveal to your pupils – let them see that you are a human being, but at the same time, focus on retaining a professional distance.

> Use humour to engage your students, or diffuse problems, but do this judiciously: don't make them think that you do not care or are not taking an issue seriously.

> Invest some energy in exploring ways of bringing your lesson content to life: simple things, like anecdotes or unusual examples, can make a considerable difference with minimal effort.

> Teachers and pupils alike feel that one of the worst crimes is being a chronically lazy, unmotivated teacher who has no passion for her/his job.

Communication skills

Teaching is all about communication. Our role involves imparting knowledge, giving instructions, building relationships, managing social behaviour and passing on information. All of these things require a sophisticated level of communication. We often talk about people having good communication skills, and it is frequently a prerequisite for fulfilling a job specification. But what does this actually mean?

Communication skills can be divided into two areas: verbal and non-verbal. Non-verbal communication is quite straightforward. It is about body language and mannerisms, and there are only so many things we can do with those. Verbal communication is perhaps the harder one to master, as we have to focus on two things at once: content *and* tone. It is about both what we say and how we say it. The real trick, of course, is to be able to use both verbal and non-verbal communication to reinforce what we are trying to express, so that the one backs up the other.

Reflection box:
Take a moment to pay attention to yourself when you are in teaching flow. How are you standing/sitting? Where are you situated? What are your hands doing? How does your voice sound? How does it feel if you alter things (e.g. stand somewhere different, speak more slowly, etc.)?

For some, effective communication is something that comes to them instinctively. For others, it is a life-long learning process – or not, as one rather disgruntled secondary teacher suggested:

> There are so many teachers that are incredibly *bad* at communicating. Either they just talk continuously, without paying attention to the needs of the pupils and the fact that they can't cope with listening for long periods of time. Or they 're just really boring . . . some teachers just drone on and on and on, and then wonder why the pupils are difficult . . . it's like they don't have any awareness of how they are affecting things.

Awareness and, particularly, self-awareness have to be key considerations for any teacher. Those in my discussion group generally agreed that they are always self-conscious of their verbal/non-verbal communication in the classroom, and although this is demanding on them, it is definitely part of what makes for 'perfect' classroom practice. Having a sense of awareness – of the atmosphere, the mood, the noise level, etc. (of both yourself and your pupils) – allows you to modify your manner accordingly, maybe to raise your game or calm things down. Without it, the dynamics of the classroom may easily spiral out of your control. As one teacher put it, when good communication is happening it seems effortless and unnoticeable; it is when it's not happening that it becomes obvious – when pupils and staff stop listening to each other, and fail to find out what is expected of them.

Awareness is also a valuable buffer between 'instinctive' responses and 'professional' responses, as noted by a Youth Worker at a school for pupils with behavioural difficulties:

> I've watched a few members of staff get really threatening and, sometimes even aggressive, in front of kids they don't get on with. They argue and end up losing it (which the kid always gets blamed for). I know everyone's human and that dealing with some of the pupils and their attitudes can be stressful, but getting angry is not professional and it's not good for anyone. They need to slow down and think before they react.

Many teachers confessed to having moments where they got carried away, and lost control of their communication skills, sometimes resulting in conflict and argument. They felt that the brief was too huge to fully manage without any hitches. Within the pressure and stresses of the day it is reasonable to expect that, at some point, people's tolerance levels will give way; but having some awareness of what this feels like, can at least help prompt you to stop and pull back, or change your approach. The emphasis should be on 'trying' and that is good enough:

> Sometimes I can feel the stress rising up in me. I can feel myself getting hotter in the face, and my heart beating, and I just want to shout and tell them all to ★★★★ off . . . and why shouldn't I? What I'm putting up with is something that most people just wouldn't stand for. But then I have that galvanising moment, that little bit of clarity, where I regain composure and pull myself together. I won't be beaten by them. It's not worth it. And I know that losing my rag will just create more problems in the long term.

Reflection box:

How do you keep your cool? List all of the things that help you to stay calm in your general life. Can they also be used in the classroom environment?

Verbal communication is hard to keep in check, because there are so many different issues to think about and consider. When asked what could help the process, responses included as follows:

Being aware of the needs of different pupils.
Being sensitive to the mood of the class, and maintaining a good rapport with pupils who are having a 'bad day'.
Being aware of speaking clearly and with structure. Keep it simple: less is more.
Regularly checking that you have been understood.
Varying your tone.
Actively listening to the class, rather than simply waiting to speak again.
Having a few stock phrases, or planned responses for difficult situations.
Observing other teachers.
Experience!

Many teachers had strong feelings about listening as part of the skill of good communication, reminding us that it is a two-way process. Effective listening requires patience and concentration in its own right. Unfortunately this is something that can be easily lost in the urge to keep the lesson momentum going, as illustrated by an anecdote from an advisory teacher.

> I once modelled a lesson in front of some new teachers. At one point I asked the class quite a complex question, and although students were clearly motivated to find the answer, they took their time – as I expected. After a while, one student called out to me in a puzzled voice, 'why have you stopped talking?' 'I'm giving you some *'thinking'* time,' I replied. They just stared at me with their mouths open. This was completely unexpected for them.

For various reasons, speaking can sometimes take precedence over listening in the classroom – teachers may feel they are under pressure to rattle through the curriculum, or will worry that if they aren't talking, their students will take the opportunity to do some talking of their own. But the 'perfect' teacher is perhaps not threatened by passing time or silence, and is not afraid of getting wrapped up in a particular discussion at the expense of remembering what they had planned to say next. That said, there is also a need to maintain the learning momentum, to feel confident and in control of where your discussion is going, and to keep the main points in focus. It is perhaps a balancing act between instinct and preparation.

Reflection box:
How comfortable are you about letting go during class discussions? Do you meticulously plan the points you want to make beforehand, or do you just wait and see where the pupils' comments and reactions take you? How does it feel to do the opposite of what you are used to?

A teacher-training lecturer suggested that the use of one's personal judgement (which takes us back to the theme of 'awareness') is another key factor in successful communication. It is not just about recognising when something is or isn't working, but about being able to apply different communication 'styles' to different situations, age groups and class sizes. For example, the manner in which a teacher addresses younger pupils could seem patronising to a group of teenagers. Or for another example, the communication requirements for dealing with a large class of pupils in a drama hall would need to be more authoritative and commanding, compared to leading an intimate lesson with a small group of individuals.

Judgement also steps in when considering the nature of the pupils. Some may respond well to a no-nonsense approach and a stern, scary voice; others may buck against this and argue back, creating bigger problems for you; or alternatively they may feel intimidated and become withdrawn. Some pupils will need to be led step-by-step through each little detail and instruction; others will grasp things quickly, and would rather go off on intellectual tangents. As I said, the brief is a broad one! It is about knowing your students, and knowing what method of communication will have the most effective impact on them. Whilst this can vary from school to school, it can also vary from class to class within the same school, and from pupil to pupil. It is the age-old dilemma of working out how to be many things to many people.

In talking to pupils, from a variety of age groups and backgrounds, it seems that they all generally hope for a teacher who is 'nice most of the time' but strict when pupils misbehave. Taking this to another level, it may be useful to think of communication as having a 'management' angle and an 'information' angle – the tone of these two aspects should be different, thus students are able to recognise when 'Miss/Sir' is wanting to share ideas, explain, have fun or inspire, and then to realise when she/he means business!

Effective communication is also about timing. When do you set homework? When do you give out instructions for a new task? It helps that the safety talk is always given out *before* the plane takes off the runway. Once the flight starts, people are distracted. They're more interested in looking out of the window, or reading or panicking. In the classroom you need to make the most of the opportunities when you have your audience at its most captive. Set homework at the start of the lesson, and never use the phrase 'lets get started then' until you are ready, and are sure that they know what it is they are starting to do – otherwise you will be forever having to repeat it.

I want to consider non-verbal communication now and think about what that involves. I was once taught by a small, soft-spoken female teacher, who was always given the most difficult pupils in the school because she had an amazing knack of pulling them into line with little more than an eyebrow raise. As soon as that eyebrow came up, they stopped whatever it was they were doing and cowered. Of course, it wasn't just the amazing powers of her eyebrow. The reason she was able to have such control was because of her ruthless consistency, which is something I shall discuss in further detail in Chapter 3, 'Dealing with discipline'; but it illustrates the point that sometimes a look, or a gesture can have as much, or even more, power than the voice itself.

The variety of non-verbal gestures that teachers said they make use of include the following:

For getting whole-class or individual attention: folding arms and looking bored/impatient, sighing, looking at watch, clearing throat, clapping hands together, blowing a whistle, ringing a reception desk bell, writing on the board a message along the lines of 'By the time you finish reading this you will be silent', writing (or pretending) to make a note of disruptive pupils names, tapping the desk, sitting down and getting out a magazine, sitting next to or in between disruptive pupils, finger on lips

For getting a pupil to stop minor misbehaviour: standing close to them and using physical proximity to make them aware that you have noticed, looking directly at them and shaking head, raising an eyebrow, waggling a finger, pointing to a classroom rules poster, writing pupil's name on board, making a hang-man gesture, walking over and placing an open hand in front of them (if you want them to hand you something they shouldn't be messing about with), using fingers to countdown

For maintaining pupil interest during group discussion: walking purposefully around room so that all pupils feel they are being observed, looking directly at the pupil whom they want to answer the questions/volunteer, using hand gestures to emphasise key points, waving/clapping hands to 'wake' pupils up, directing teaching towards lazy pupils

It is important to keep body language and physical actions congruent with verbal language. If your mouth is saying one thing ('Class! Stop talking!'), but your body is saying another (eyes darting about all over the place, hiding behind the desk, nervously chewing fingernails) the message is diluted. Likewise, if you are standing firmly upfront with your hands on your hips, but your pitch is raised and your voice is tailing off, your pupils may not take your intentions seriously.

Reflection box:
Practice in front of a mirror saying the same words but with different tones of voice, different pitch and different eye contact. Vary your physical stance and mannerism, to see how they affect things. Can you say the same words but convey different meanings?

Key points for communication:

> Effective communication involves verbal and non-verbal signals (what we say and what we do).
> For maximum effect, make sure the two reflect and reinforce one another.
> Be aware of your style and patterns of communication, and be ready to adjust them if necessary.
> Develop a range of non-verbal gestures to convey your intentions, whilst saving your voice.
> Think of verbal communication in terms of *what* you say and *how* you say it.
> Vary your tone and pitch to keep pupils interested.
> Remember to take time to listen.
> Keep instructions simple, so that the key points don't get lost.
> Effective communication is a skill that *can* be learned. It just requires practice.

Relationships with pupils

Your efforts to build positive relationships with pupils can have a significant impact on the classroom. I know this from my own experiences of working with extremely challenging young people: individuals who had lots of mistrust and dislike for all things educational (including teachers!). Building trust and establishing that sense of mutual 'respect' was the only way we could move forward to the point where lessons actually looked like lessons and the curriculum could be taught. It was a long and frustrating but ultimately worthwhile experience.

The value of building positive relationships with pupils is highlighted by a head teacher, who regards it as a prerequisite for 'perfect' teaching:

> The least I can hope for when looking for effective members of a teaching team, is those who are able to build some kind of rapport with the pupils. It's from this rapport that everything else flows.

Pupil/teacher relationships have an impact on everything, from behavioural issues to academic motivation. So what makes for the 'perfect' pupil/teacher relationship? How does one establish that all-important rapport? Judging by their feedback, younger children are on the lookout for someone who can:

Make them feel safe
Help them sort out their difficulties
Make learning fun

Older children and secondary age pupils also seem to want the added bonus of teachers who do not patronise them, who are fair and who treat classes with respect. One recent school leaver had some vitriolic but somewhat enlightening thoughts on the issue:

> Most of the teachers at my school were either too thick, or too old-fashioned and stuffy, and the rest were not much older than me and were sometimes quite nasty. They didn't like non-conformity and were totally set in their ways. It seemed like their whole focus was on getting pupils to conform in class, and anyone who was 'different' got picked on. It didn't matter whether they were causing trouble or not . . . there was one that we liked: she was fun and knew her stuff, and was quite accepting of different people.

> **Reflection box:**
> How do you think your pupils would describe their relationship with you? Would you dare to ask them?

A number of suggestions were made, regarding how to build a rapport with students, and thankfully none of them involve being young, attractive and incredibly cool:

- Make an effort to get to know them: ask them about their interests, for example musical tastes, sport, hobbies, family, etc.
- Remember what these things are, and whenever possible, ask questions or engage them in conversation (e.g. 'What did you think of the match last night?'). This implies that you value and listen to what they tell you.
- Avoid pre-judging, making assumptions or basing your opinion on a student's reputation before you have spent some time with them yourself.
- Welcome pupils into your classroom and smile!
- Express your own enthusiasm for your lessons and your subject. If they see that it matters to you they will know that you care.
- Follow things up: if you say you'll do something then make sure you do it, so that pupils maintain their faith in you. For instance, if you promise them a trip or reward, or if you are setting a sanction, they need to see that you are true to your word.
- Be consistent and reliable in your approach and mannerisms, so that pupils know they can trust and feel secure around you.
- Notice effort and improvement.
- Be careful not to appear too dismissive of things, for example, arguments or silly name-calling. Whilst these issues may not be important (or convenient) to you, they may be of greater significance to your pupils.
- Make pupils feel that they genuinely matter. Express positive belief in their potential and their achievements. Give deserving praise where it's earned.

Although a handful teachers held on to the principle that 'teachers are not there to be liked', generally people had a unified response to the question of whether teachers should aim to be friends or foes to their classes. They felt that it was wise to avoid either extreme, and to find a balance between making the class a welcoming place and establishing clear authority. As has previously been suggested, an effective way of finding this balance is through being firm with the whole-class and firm with the rules, but friendly with individuals; giving pupils the hint that you are a pleasant, likeable person, someone worth being on the right side of.

As pupils get older, it seems they become increasingly cynical towards the teacher-as-friend concept. A group of sixth formers I talked to were keen to explain their frustrations regarding certain staff members who behaved in this way:

> He thinks he is the most popular teacher in the school, because he jokes around and his lessons are a laugh. Two years ago, we had him for History and we thought he was amazing, but now we're doing our A level's, we've got loads of work to do, and we don't want to muck about. I'm fed up of talking about his local pub, or waiting months to get my coursework marked. I don't want to be his 'mate'. I just want good A level results.

Comments such as this highlight the pitfalls of being what some may describe as a 'cool' teacher. Yes, it may win a class over in the short term, but what happens when deadlines start to whiz by and requests for coursework are met with a flippant: 'Ow sir, what are you moaning for? You're normally a laugh . . .' When I meet teachers of this ilk, if I'm honest, I find myself wondering whether their popularity tactics say more about their personal issues, than their professional ones. The 'perfect' teacher, of course, would not need to rely on the popularity vote to know and understand their worth in the classroom. A secondary school deputy head remarked:

> Friend or foe? You should be neither. Any tendency towards one or the other is wrong. You are not their enemy, but nor are you their friend. You are their mentor – you are there to oversee their learning, and this responsibility must not be forgotten.

This argument brings us back to the question of respect – the middle ground. Given that everyone acknowledges its importance in the classroom, which therefore implies that it is a perfect teacher staple, how do we go about establishing it? What does a respectful relationship look like?

> Respect is quite an intangible thing. Partly, it's about being there, turning up on time, being consistent with the way you deal with things, expressing support for them, knowing their names . . . I guess I'm saying it's about doing all the things that you'd expect them to do for you.

This point, made by an NQT, reminds us that respect is very much a two-way process – if we want it from our pupils, then we need to give it in return. There is little room in the classroom for hypocrisy. Much of my discussions with pupils, parents and teachers revealed that young people have a very strong sense of what they perceive as fair. It matters significantly that everyone is treated as equal, and that if there are any discrepancies in the way a teacher deals with pupils, the reasons 'why' are clearly explained to them. In other words, pupils want some kind of transparency, or honesty from their teachers.

They also want, as has been suggested, their teachers to set the example. A parent I spoke to, illustrated this expectation with her own personal experience:

> My son got a detention for arriving late to a music lesson, even though he'd been helping another pupil who had had an upset. I was cross about this, because I knew that he was only trying to do the right thing, and wasn't mucking about. When I probed him a bit more, he explained that he hadn't thought turning up late would be such a problem, because the music teacher in question was regularly arriving up to twenty minutes late – the class would be left standing outside, and some of the students would wander off, or just muck about whilst they were waiting! I complained to the school because I think this is unacceptable, and sets a terrible example.

Establishing a relationship of respect is, of course, not just about modelling desired behaviour, but about presenting yourself as someone whose opinions and expectations matter. A primary head teacher suggests:

> Classroom respect is created through the understanding that one is the teacher and one is the learner – and that each side understands and accepts these roles. As the teacher, you can reinforce this by ensuring that you are consistent, that you have a good command of your knowledge and that you value the learning above everything else. You need to show them that you care about their achievements, and that you want to see them fulfil themselves as human beings and as learners.

However, as was stated at the start of this book, different schools can, by the nature of their location, size, pupil intake, etc, have different agendas. So the question of how to gain respect cannot have one simple 'this is all you have to do' response. In contrast to the previous quote, a behaviour support teacher working in a so-called 'tough' school suggested that respectful classroom relationships are closely linked to behaviour and attitude rather than directly to the learning process:

> I believe in purposeful control as opposed to control for control's sake. If you want your pupils to respect you, you need to ensure that you are seen as the centre of attention – not necessarily the authority figure or the big bully – but the locus of control within the class and the central figure, to whom everyone looks for guidance. If you want their respect you need to exude confidence, even if you don't feel it inside, because you need to promote the idea that you are a leader. You need them to feel that they can trust and rely upon you to sort things if problems arise.

Reflection box:
Is respect on the agenda in your classroom? How do you go about showing pupils that you deserve their respect? Do you and them have a common understanding of what respect is?

So is it okay to have favourite pupils within the class? Yes, we know that the perfect teacher needs to be consistent, and should treat everyone as fairly as possible, but we are only human, after all. Generally, teachers felt that it would be unnatural not to have favourites, but that it was necessary to be discreet about it. Responses included: 'having favourites is what keeps you going', 'have them but don't let anyone know', and 'aim for every pupil to *think* that they are your favourite'.

And as for the kind of pupils that teachers felt that were drawn to or enjoyed working with, answers ranged from: 'the naughty ones', 'the ones who are funny and cheeky', 'the ones who need me the most', 'the ones who have sharp wit and intelligence', and 'not necessarily the cleverest or most well-behaved, but the ones who have that "spark"'. One secondary Informations and Communications Technology (ICT) teacher pointed out:

> When I discussed some of the pupils that I thought were really great with a PE teacher at my school, he hadn't ever noticed them. To him they were the weedy lads who hid at the back of the football pitch. But to me, they were funny and talented – they were the ones who stood out.

Everybody has somebody – hopefully. So what about the pupils that make it hard for us to like them? At the top of the list, not surprisingly, came the 'nasty', bullying types and the ones that upset other pupils. One teacher suggested that when she comes across these individuals, she has to keep reminding herself that they are behaving that way because they may have had unpleasant experiences themselves, or may come from dysfunctional homes. Other examples included pupils who intimidate or try to take over from the teacher; or the sneaky, manipulative one, those who start trouble and then just sit back and enjoy the chaos.

Naturally, positive relationships with pupils are things that develop over time. For staff who remain in the same school for many years, there is definitely something special in being able to see little tiny first years through their entire primary/secondary education and out of the other side. Time also allows staff and pupils to develop trust in each other, and to establish an instinctive understanding of what the other needs, or expects. Perhaps the 'perfect' teacher would do well to stick in one job and one school for a period of time, so that both they and their pupils can benefit from a deeper bond.

This point is echoed by the experience of a primary supply teacher who described how:

> I'd taken a post doing one term with a class before I went back to my native New Zealand. This class hadn't had a permanent teacher for the whole year, and consequently they were quite unsettled. A lot of supply teachers didn't stick with them for more then a few weeks, because they found them too challenging. Towards the end of my term with them, they really improved and were lovely. But as soon as I told them I was leaving, they turned on me – I don't blame them. They obviously felt let down . . . again.

Inevitably, the benefits of building positive relationships with pupils are difficult to achieve if you work as a supply teacher, or for various reasons such as timetabling, have limited long-term interaction with the same students. Another London-based supply teacher explained:

> If you go from school to school you are often a sitting target – although you may not care anyway, because you know it's easy to walk away. From my experience, I would say it helps to create links with a few schools or to get long-term placements. Otherwise it's tough as a supply teacher, especially in secondary schools.

So what can you do?

> Either you win them over by force of personality. It helps if you are one of those big booming voice, big physical presence types. Alternatively, you can make the most of engaging activities that have an immediate impact.

I have always thought that one of the best examples of a great supply teacher was the one Lisa Simpson (of the 'The Simpsons' cartoon) had. This chap did away with the work he was supposed to do with the class, which would have had them climbing the walls, and did something inspiring about cowboys. It didn't matter that it was out of context; the point was, he got the class learning and enjoying learning.

Key points for relationships with pupils:

> Focus on building a positive, respectful rapport with your classes.
> Avoid leaning to the extremes of being a 'friend' to your pupils, or an 'enemy'.
> Try to be firm with rules and expectations, and friendly towards individuals, and enthusiastic about learning.
> Aim for fair treatment of pupils, and be prepared to justify your decisions.
> Show pupils that you *care* about them and their learning, by having high expectations, and giving regular encouragement and praise.
> Lead by example: don't expect pupils to follow rules that you aren't prepared to adhere to yourself.
> Have favourites (but be discreet about it)!
> Remember that trusting and 'instinctive' relationships develop over time – stick with it!
> Never be afraid to assert boundaries where necessary, even if you are worried that your good relationships will suffer; pupils will respect you more if you assert your leadership of the class (if they have done something wrong, they will probably expect to be called up for it).

Assertiveness and self-confidence

Feeling self-assured is a valuable trait in any walk of life, but a career in teaching can really put this to the test. When you stand up in front of a class, whether it is for the first time in your life or the last, you are placing yourself under the spotlight. There may be up to 30 different faces all staring back at you, watching, wondering, waiting and possibly looking for ways in which they can challenge you. It is more than likely that you will be on your own in that classroom, so it is down to you to keep order, to make sure that you are getting everyone interested and on-task, and to present yourself as a calm, in-control leader. Sounds scary, doesn't it?

Given that we already know that 'perfect' teaching requires a bit of dynamism, as well as clear, confident communication skills, an assertive personality is inevitably an asset in the classroom. But is every person enrolling on teacher training assertive? Is every teacher currently working in your school assertive? Probably not.

Unfortunately, life's ups and downs can take their toll on our confidence levels, whilst some people are naturally more passive than others. Of course, this doesn't mean they will automatically make bad teachers, but it may make things harder.

The sound piece of advice, which emerges time and time again, is that experience makes it easier. Of course, there is only one way to gain experience and that is by simply getting on with the job. Many teachers, when reflecting back on their careers, say that they would never want to go through the first few years again! Which isn't good news for new teachers, but is at least reassurance that the struggle will pay off.

> Last year, whilst I was training, I felt a lot more confident. I think this was because I didn't feel like I had too much on my shoulders. I was only a student, so I had an excuse if things went wrong. Plus I had lots of support from my college and mentors. Now I'm in a new school, in my first proper job and I feel like I've been thrown into the shark pit. It seems like so much more is expected of me, yet I don't feel ready for all the responsibility and I feel like I'm always making mistakes. Fortunately, my colleagues are very nice and they tell me not to worry. I look forward to next year, when I will have properly settled in and got to know the students.

Reflection box:
How far have you come? Look back over your first few years/ terms/weeks in teaching. Can you remember how it felt to stand in front of a class for the first time? Has it become easier? How much more confident do you feel? Has your experience as a teacher helped you to become more confident and assertive in general?

When asked whether it is possible to fake confidence and assertiveness in the classroom, because let's face it, we all have our dodgy days, many people confessed that they fake it all the time! One teacher explained:

> I suppose its easier if you genuinely believe in yourself and your powers, but some days I turn up at school and I've got

everything on my mind and I just think . . . uh, how am I going to cope with this? Usually I get through it. I just switch on 'teacher mode' and the kids have no idea that, inside, I'm a complete wreck. My colleagues are all the same and we joke about it. The trouble is, it does keep me awake at night, worrying that I'm really not good enough.

The curse of perfectionism. Curiously, it seems that the teaching profession attracts a good deal of individuals who would describe themselves as 'perfectionists'. Yet it is a job in which singular 'perfection', as this book attests to, is an extraordinarily difficult thing to achieve. And if high personal expectations are too frequently not achieved (often through no fault of the teacher's own), confidence levels may take a battering, leading to stress and self-doubt. Working as an advisory behaviour support teacher, much of my time was spent reassuring very good teachers that they were actually very good. Many of them had lost sight of what a happy, healthy classroom looks like. They were consumed by the battle to be 'perfect', and felt that every little class problem was due to their failure.

When asked what had helped them to develop self-confidence and assertiveness, the teachers in my discussion group suggested:

Experience
Knowing the class
Supportive colleagues
Praise and encouragement from management
Pupil success
Positive feedback from parents
Taking risks and getting positive results
Quality training
Learning to have reasonable expectations of yourself
Getting on top of organisational and paperwork matters
Knowing what you want and setting fair goals for yourself
Attending a course in assertiveness
Being able to accept mistakes and learn from them
Counselling
Change of jobs

The last point was made by a London teacher who confided that his experience in one particular school was so awful, he convinced himself he was not cut out for teaching. Demoralised, he eventually quit, but still in need of an income, he took a short-term supply job at a small special needs school, expecting to feel the same sense of dread. Instead he discovered that he fitted in really well, had a natural affinity with the pupils, and took up a full-time post. His situation is echoed by the thoughts of an ex-deputy head and school governor:

> I've worked in, and supported, many schools in my area. It's easy to tell whether a place is working or not, and whether staff feel happy and confident. It's in the atmosphere. If teachers find a school that they like, be that because of the camaraderie between staff, the spirit of the pupils, or the overall ethos of the school, they tend to stay there. And that stability makes the team even stronger. If someone doesn't fit in, they generally don't hang around . . . and that's probably to everyone's benefit.

When considering the issue of classroom confidence, it is important to recognise the difference between assertiveness, aggressiveness and passiveness. Aggressive people tend to try and dominate others, or use force to get their way. Although this is clearly a dubious way to manage a classroom situation, it is still apparent in schools everywhere. We have all encountered staff members who rule through fear. Their quiet classrooms and impeccably behaved students may seem impressive at first glance, but the hidden side of it can be negative. This is what one sixth-form student had to say:

> If you have ever been bullied by a teacher, you will understand how destructive it is. When I was in my last year of primary school, we had a teacher who was really strict, but she was also quite nasty with it. She would make us stand up in front of the whole class if we made a mistake, and if someone so much as turned around in their seat, she would scream at them. It was horrible, really. In that year I became quite shy and I tried to avoid going to school, because I was scared of getting into trouble with her – even though I was one of the well-behaved ones . . . I don't think I learnt much either, I was too busy worrying.

In contrast, passive people are submissive to others and may allow themselves to be 'walked all over'. In the classroom, this can obviously lead to trouble, with pupils dictating the direction of their lessons, as one teacher laments:

> In my last school, I felt quite intimidated by the pupils . . . there was one class that got really out of control. To be honest, I think it was my own fault, because I just didn't assert myself. I was frightened to say anything, because I didn't want to create more grief for myself. They used to say, 'We'll only be quiet if we can do this or that', and I used to let them. Ironically, a few of the pupils came up to me in the corridor and said, 'We're bored – why don't make us do some work?'

So the ideal is to tread somewhere down the middle, and that's where assertiveness comes in: those who know what they want and stand up for themselves, but without feeling the need to intimidate or use bully tactics. A learning mentor highlighted the value of this approach:

> It sets a good example to the students. There are so many negative influences around, in music, sport and television. I think young people are given the impression that aggressive, predatory behaviour is the way to stay on top, and that staying on top, being number one, is the most important thing. If you're not on top, or able to stick up for yourself, then you're perceived as weak. I meet so many kids who have very low self-esteem, so it's important that they have role models who can show them that you don't have to be a bully, or a victim; you just have to be true to yourself.

Reflection box:
Do you see yourself as passive? Aggressive? Or assertive? How do you think others, including your pupils, see you? If being assertive is the most desirable and effective of the three, what would help you to feel more like this?

Key points for assertiveness and self-confidence:
> Understand the difference between assertive, aggressive and passive behaviour and identify what best describes you and how you can make it work in your classroom.
> Assertive behaviour is the most effective and most desired approach.
> If in doubt, or if you are having a bad day, remember that assertive behaviour and outward confidence are often 'faked' (see section on Teacher personality).
> Experience helps.
> Underpin your self-confidence by deciding what your personal classroom values are, and sticking up for them.
> Remember that pupils want boundaries so don't be afraid to assert them. Having a planned response for pupils that resist (see Chapter 3 on Dealing with discipline) can reduce the anxiety of possible conflict.
> Training can enhance or provide new skills, and give you a confidence boost.
> Recognise that low self-confidence can be changed, but that you may need some help to do this, for example, support from colleagues, friends and family or counselling.

2 Making learning happen

Subject knowledge

Good subject knowledge is a desirable 'perfect teacher' quality. It could perhaps be argued that all teaching starts with the teacher's own knowledge. Their role is to impart their experience, understanding and skill onto others, so how well informed they are will inevitably shape the quality and breadth of the learning opportunities they can provide. The initial question I posed to teachers was: what is more important for your subject, enthusiasm or in-depth knowledge?

The consensus was that enthusiasm mattered most. One senior teacher and curriculum coordinator explained:

> Enthusiasm is definitely more important. You can always acquire knowledge as you go, but if you can't generate enthusiasm for your subject you will struggle. A good teacher is not simply a repository of dry information; their aim should be to bring that information to life.

A retired teacher further explained the need to like and care about the subject matter:

> When it was something I was personally interested in, I was so much better at getting it over to the pupils. The insights would be more meaningful and the discussion would go further. It would feel like I was benefiting, and gaining from the experience, as well as them – and I think that is a good culture of learning to have. Even though I'm now retired, I still see or read things and think, oh, I could make a good lesson out of that!

With able and older pupils, having confidence in your subject knowledge becomes increasingly important:

> With younger classes, you can often bluff your way through an unfamiliar topic, because the level of work isn't so demanding. With my sixth form group, however, they expect me to know more than they do, and will sometimes ask some very searching, perceptive questions, which keep me on my toes. I like the challenge, but if I haven't had the chance to prepare properly, I feel quite nervous going into the lesson. I worry that they will catch me out.

But surely a 'perfect' teacher wouldn't have to bluff her/his way through anything? Perfect teachers would be impeccably prepared for all eventualities – in an ideal world perhaps. A number of teachers explained that they had, or were having, to teach subjects that they had little knowledge of in the first place, through no fault of their own. This is especially an issue for primary school teachers, who have a broad spectrum of subjects to cover, but it can also be an issue for secondary school teachers:

> I trained as a PE and Dance specialist, but I now seem to spend half my timetable making up for gaps in the workforce. I currently teach Year 7 and 8 Art and Design and Year 7 ICT. It's not ideal, because I hate computers, and I am having to do lots of additional work just to keep up with the pupils – most of them know more than I do.

Teachers in similar situations all agreed that research and preparation, although time-consuming, is vital. Staying ahead is not too difficult if you plan what you are doing in advance, and if you work through medium/long-term plans (i.e. the term or year's topics planned out from the start of the academic year) you will be able to gather useful ideas and activities for upcoming projects well in advance. Nevertheless, it would be unrealistic to expect that the gentle art of bluff doesn't come into it at any point – why bluff is a skill in itself!

Reflection box:
How do you manage pupil questions that you don't know the answer to? Do you brush them off, make up an answer, or explain that you're not sure and will get back to them?

A teacher from Leeds suggested that advances in technology have had a fortunate affect on the limits of his subject knowledge:

> My subject (History) is very broad. I spent a lot of time at University focusing on one small aspect of it, so it is difficult to have an answer for everything. Every now and then, a student will ask me something that I don't have a ready answer for. I'm not afraid to admit not knowing, but I never like to leave a question unanswered, whatever it's about, because that's where I can make a difference. Last week, someone asked me about the Petronas Towers in Kuala Lumpur, so we looked them up, there and then, using the Internet on the interactive whiteboard. It was slightly off subject, but everyone learned something.

For teachers of Sciences, Arts or any subject where practical activities are involved, prior background knowledge and understanding of how a particular demonstration, experiment or project will work can be invaluable. A Design and Technology teacher explained:

> Whenever I am about to start a new project, I always do it myself beforehand. This means I then have a tangible example to show the class, but more importantly, it reminds me of what can go wrong, or what I need to get pupils to look out for when they are doing the work themselves. If I didn't do this, I reckon half of my projects would end up in disaster!

So where do teachers get their ideas, resources and information from? The following list is by no means exhaustive, but it does throw up some unexpected practice: several teachers claimed to find inspiration for lesson ideas whilst away on holiday! Surely there are better things to do! Other ideas included the following:

Internet searches
Text books
From personal reading
Own imagination
The media: TV, radio, magazines, newspapers
Relating things to pupils' own lives and interests
Topical references (e.g. Eastenders, the latest scandal, football)
Libraries
Other teachers
INSET and training courses
Previous projects or lesson plans
Internet-generated lesson plans
On holiday
QCA and National Curriculum documents

There was a definite sense of indifference towards the National Curriculum, although a few suggested that it had a focusing effect on their teaching:

It stops you from being too self-indulgent and pulls you up on areas you might be weak on. As an English teacher, I'm not wild about teaching grammar, but the National Curriculum makes me address it, otherwise I may be tempted to neglect it. The National Curriculum is a security blanket, and some kids benefit from that sort of structure.

Others felt it was too restrictive for both themselves and for their pupils. They didn't want it on a plate. They wanted more opportunity to exercise their individual skill and creativity within the classroom. Many suggested they would prefer a return to a topic-based approach, which would allow pupils to be immersed in a particular theme or idea over a consistent period of time, and would enable the teacher to provide a more satisfying and enriching learning experience.

From a parent's perspective, the general concern, understandably, was that their children were getting the education they required. For most, the expectation was that pupils were being provided with the National Curriculum and working towards exams, with the feeling that teachers had a responsibility to help their children gain the grades that would safe-guard their future. However, many parents also raised the concern that they would not want their children to be mere slaves to exam results:

> What if my daughter left school with good exam grades, but with an absolute hatred for poetry, or reading? I want her to be taught the National Curriculum if that's what she needs, but there still needs to be some allowance for more experimental, adventurous learning.

For the 'perfect' teacher, reconciling the two can present quite a challenge: on the one hand, addressing the curriculum requirements and preparing pupils for coursework/exams/testing, on the other, being free and creative and inspirational – which can sometimes require a lot of pondering and head scratching. Simply fitting in the basics can be a feat in itself, so perhaps it is best to start with these and then work out how you can deliver them imaginatively and creatively. And this doesn't have to be done alone. Sitting down with colleagues for a brainstorming session will help to share the burden and can generate lots of different ideas.

Reflection box:
How many opportunities do you get to plan/share ideas with colleagues? How much time do you spend struggling to think of new and exciting lesson ideas?

Key points for subject knowledge:
> - Enthusiasm counts: look out for tasks and themes that grab your own interest.
> - Keep a small notebook handy wherever you go, you never know when a lesson idea might strike!
> - Preparation is key: prior research will give you added confidence, and with modern technology this does not need to be unnecessarily time-consuming.

> When teaching practical or complicated tasks, take time to work through the activity yourself, so that you can make sure your instructions are adequate, and can be modified in case of problems.
> Wherever possible, find a balance between addressing the demands of the curriculum, and creating opportunities for more adventurous learning.
> Use your colleagues: sharing ideas, skills and plans can alleviate the pressure on yourself.

Planning and preparation

How much time does the 'perfect' teacher spend planning and preparing her/his lessons? Perhaps the simple answer is 'as much as they *need* to'. No more. No less. This amount will depend on the type of lesson being taught, the range of pupil abilities within the class, and the teacher's level of experience. And, of course, all of this is wrapped up within that age-old limitation: time.

It would be unwise to suggest that the perfect teacher needs to dedicate many hours of their week to producing immaculate, detailed lesson plans; and the rest of their spare time organising elaborate, impressive resources. This is possibly somebody's idea of perfection, but for most of us it is an unrealistic aim, and does not necessarily equate to an effective classroom performance. Looking back on his experiences as a trainee teacher, one primary teacher explained:

> I used to spend several hours every evening, writing up my lesson plans for the following day. They were four pages long, and I was paranoid that if I left any information out, I would fail the course. And then on top of that, I would sit up till two in the morning, making stuff that I could use in my lessons, convinced that if I didn't produce something amazing for every subject, the pupils would just muck about . . . when it came to delivering the actual lessons, I was so tired I could barely speak!

A good lesson plan should be a working document, something that supports what happens in the classroom, serving as a guide or prompt for the teacher, but without stifling the actual experience of teaching. In several discussions the idea of 'instinct' came up, with teachers considering the extent to which their lesson content reflected their planning. Opinions differed, so I shall highlight some of the key thoughts.

Reflection box:

How long do you spend preparing lesson plans each day/week/term? Can you fit this work into your school day or do you have to take work home or do it at the weekend? Do you feel that this amount of time spent on planning is in appropriate ratio to the amount of time spent actually teaching the lessons?

An NQT explained: 'My planning gives me security. It takes up a lot of my time, but without it, I would feel very ill equipped to face a class . . . I like to include seating plans, timings, and little prompts about what I need to say to the class. Sometimes, I even rehearse the night before. I know it seems ridiculous, but it gives me reassurance. When I get to the class, I'm word perfect!'

In contrast, an experienced special needs teacher argued: 'I'm what you'd call an 'old hand' . . . I know my students and my lessons inside and out, so I'm able to go with the flow. Planning involves jotting down some notes on the back of an envelope – if you're lucky . . . It's more important to me to spend my time making resources and organising activities that really benefit the children, rather than filling in little boxes for *them* (meaning government school inspectors)!'

Resentment such as this, the frustrations of excessive paperwork and government 'tick boxes', was echoed by many others – particularly the more experienced teachers. I also heard talk of the myth of the OFSTED proof lesson plan – the one that secures their favour. However, the school inspector's line is that they do not require a particular format for lesson plans and are simply expecting to see evidence of good planning, in line with the school's planning requirements.

Perhaps planning means different things to different people, depending on where they are in their careers. For inexperienced teachers and those that are newly qualified, a lesson plan can represent a security blanket; a way of structuring and clarifying what can otherwise seem like a daunting process. For more experienced teachers, however, who are able to rely increasingly on instinct and prior experience of what does/does not work in the classroom, writing lesson plans may feel like a treadmill. One of the cruellest aspects of this treadmill is the fact that time spent writing plans and/or preparing wonderful lesson resources can sometimes come to very little. There are no guarantees that a well-crafted lesson will not be destroyed by an unexpected fire alarm, or wasp invasion!

Reflection box:
Do you dare to do the opposite of what you are used to? Experiment by trying to teach a lesson without any plan whatsoever, or alternatively, by following one precisely. How does it feel? How do the pupils react? Is it easier or harder than you thought it would be? Are there any benefits to be had?

The key is to make sure that whatever planning you do has purpose – that it enables you to be more organised, more focused and, therefore, more effective in the classroom. Certainly, from my experience I have learned that effective planning makes me a better teacher, and it also leads to calmer, happier pupils, who benefit from the sense of structure it creates. It is, however, a personalised process: simple and succinct, but messy: full of codes and shorthand and, sometimes, even diagrams – because for me, that represents the quickest and most effective way to make sense of what is in my head. Perhaps the secret to successful planning is to find out what works for you, because not everyone finds the same things useful. If this, in turn, is balanced with the information required by your school/training college (which is hopefully reasonable), then hey presto, that's a lesson plan!

Hints and ideas on what can be effective are abundant. Here are some suggestions:

  Use a uniform format/planning sheet that is easy to fill in (either by hand or on computer) and easy to interpret, should anyone else need to teach from your plan
  Or use a spiral bound Teacher's Planner, preferably one that is specific to your school's timetable, so that you have a different box for each lesson

Divide planning into long/medium (topics for the year or term) and short term (a break down of each individual lesson), so that you are able to prepare ahead of yourself

Focus on lesson aims and objectives and keep reminding yourself of these, so that the focus of your plan remains clear

Save time by taking aims and objectives directly from National Curriculum and QCA documents, which are available online

Alternatively, use these as your plans, using post-its/annotations to show where you have adapted work to suit the needs of your pupils

Consider pupil assessment in your planning, so that you can be sure that they are working within their capabilities as well as being stretched: what do they already know and what do they need to know next?

Don't over-rely on text books/course books, which can help inform planning, but cannot replace a teacher's own ideas and instincts

Get together with other staff for group planning sessions, or to make sure you are not repeating plans that might already exist

Ensure that lessons plans are filed and kept together in one place, so that they are easily accessed should anyone request to see them

Don't throw plans away, as they can be recycled and adapted for future class groups

There is some suggestion that teachers should be wary of over-relying on their planning, which returns to the idea of teachers having 'instinct'. Whilst effective planning can clearly be an asset, the 'perfect' teacher would still need to let go of it at times, to be flexible, and, as the self-confessed 'old hand' put it, 'go with the flow':

Sometimes pupils get really into something, or they surprise me by showing an interest in a part of the lesson that I hadn't expected them to. I would never want to restrict that, because that shows a natural curiosity for what's going on. I'd happily throw out the plan, or skip part of a lesson, in order to take an idea and run with it.

Reflection box:

To what extent do your lessons represent what is in your lesson plans? Do you stick to them rigidly, or do you stray down other avenues? Is your commitment (or non-commitment) to your plans affected by other factors, for example your relationship with the class, your confidence and interest in the subject/topic?

As has been previously stated, there is no prescribed format or length for lesson plans. OFSTED simply specifies that 'teachers plan effectively, using clear objectives that children understand'. So why do so many teachers feel compelled to conjure up a one-off spectacular when the inspectors come calling? One primary head teacher offers reassurance:

Planning is important, but I don't want people to feel under obligation. If you are a good teacher, that demonstrates itself in your practice – it's not about being meticulous in your paper-work. If a member of staff were to come to me complaining about planning, I would tell them that it's not a problem to me, but that it still has to be done as a uniform requirement. These things are forced upon us, so we need to support each other. There is also something to be said for accountability.

Key points for planning and preparation:
> Develop a system that works for you and includes information that you will find useful, but also reflects your school/departmental guidelines
> Work in collaboration with colleagues, to establish a planning format, brainstorm ideas, and/or divide the planning between you
> If you are new to teaching, and are feeling overwhelmed by the time it takes for you to plan, remember that it becomes easier with experience
> Create shortcuts where possible: use a planning template, and ICT, so that certain information can be 'cut and pasted', or photocopied
> File and keep your plans, so that you don't have to repeat work

> Focus on aspects of planning that will have a direct impact on the quality of the teaching and learning in your classroom; anything else is not worth spending time on
> Do not spend 30 minutes planning a task that will last only 20!
> Plan to be flexible – include ideas for extension activities or alternative tasks, in case things don't go as expected

Lesson content, style and pace

The exact ingredients of a 'perfect' lesson are hard to quantify, as they inevitably vary according to subject, age group, class size and the nature of the pupils themselves. But after discussions with teaching staff from a number of backgrounds, it seems that, although there are a number of differences that can be identified, there are also many consistencies. This section draws these findings together.

So what does the 'perfect' teacher need to do in order to provide learning experiences that are enriching and meaningful? Perhaps the best place to start is with some key questions:

1. Is the subject matter relevant to the curriculum?
2. Are the tasks appropriate for the ability of the pupils?
3. Are the necessary resources available?
4. Is it interesting?

The issue of work being interesting is a priority concern, and for good reason. Many teachers suggested that, unless the work has some appeal to pupils, getting them motivated to do it can become an obstacle in itself. A behaviour support teacher explained:

I make sure I have a really bold beginning. I need their attention from the start because pulling them in later on is very tough. I work with really difficult, unmotivated teenagers and if something doesn't go well straight away, it's hard to salvage. But I have to judge it carefully – I can't do something so wacky that it will just lead to anarchy . . . and I MUST know my class and know what presses their buttons. That is the most essential part.

Lesson beginnings were highlighted as a key area for consideration. The initial greeting and introduction to the lesson sets the tone for the rest of it. For the teacher, it is the prime opportunity to make an impression on the pupils, to grab their attention and interest, and get them engaged. Obviously, there may be other concerns at the beginning of the lesson such as organisation and behaviour. These will be considered elsewhere in this book, but for now, let us focus on the learning.

Reflection box:
What do you do to engage pupil interest and expectation at the start of a lesson/task? Try to imagine yourself as one of your pupils – how appealing and meaningful does the work seem? Are the expectations clear?

Several teachers suggested that a useful starting point would be to have the lesson objectives written up on the board, and some expected their pupils to copy these objectives into their exercise books:

> They know what is expected of them when they come into my classroom. They sit down, sort out their bags, take out their books and begin copying the date, lesson title and objectives down. It may not be very adventurous, but it creates a clear, ordered start to each session and gets them thinking about what they are going to be doing next. I phrase the objectives as questions, for example: can I measure the area of a rectangle?

But not everyone felt this was the way to go:

> Objectives on the board – it's the OFSTED mantra. Write them up and then you'll be okay . . . but is that what teaching is all about, being okay? And just because pupils are writing them out, doesn't mean they're taking them in. Sometimes I think it's better when they don't know what's coming next. Learning should be like a voyage of discovery.

It seems that the teaching population is in danger of dividing into those who wear the badge and those who don't! Perhaps the thoughts of a London secondary school pupil will draw a line under the matter:

All of our teachers write the objectives, and some make us copy them out. (Does it help you to understand the lesson?) That depends. In some lessons the objectives are simple and the teacher is good, so it's easy to see what the point of the work is going to be; but in others, our teachers write these really boring, complicated objectives, and no one bothers to copy them down, even though we're supposed to, so they don't really help at all.

Like so many aspects of classroom practice, writing lesson objectives on the board is only as effective as the rest of your teaching. It isn't a panacea – there are no one-off magic-wand techniques in the classroom. If you teach with enthusiasm, show that you care, and work to develop that all-important rapport with your pupils, lesson objectives will be valued and digested. If you omit the above, all but the diligent few will be likely to ignore them.

The 'perfect' teacher needs to have an instinct for the job, a special something that cannot easily be quantified by techniques, tips and processes.

Naturally, this also calls into question the idea that the steps towards a 'perfect' lesson can be measured and explained. When I raised the point with my discussion groups, it caused some consternation. Some teachers felt that a heavily structured approach, including certain key features, perhaps akin to what they had been taught to do in training college, was definitely beneficial. These included as follows:

- Having a clear, structured beginning, outlying learning aims and key questions
- Opportunities for reflection and peer/self assessment of what has been learned
- Opportunities for pupils to use different learning skills (listening, discussion, problem solving, reading, group work, individual work)
- Energetic pace
- Appropriate use of ICT
- Good use of resources

- Opportunities for pupils to ask questions
- Extension activities and additional tasks to challenge the more able students
- Differentiated activities for pupils with special educational needs (SEN)
- Opportunities for pupils not only to experience success but also to be stretched
- A clear plenary and structured conclusion to the lesson

Of course, these suggestions create an utterly sound basis for any lesson, but do they create a 'perfect' one? Some teachers argued that, although a formulaic approach may be a useful support, particularly to inexperienced teachers, it actually sucks the creativity out of the craft:

> I'm not suggesting that aims and assessments are not important, but they shouldn't be focused on at the expense of genuine quality teaching. If every lesson is delivered with the same formula, where does that leave inspiration and awe? I don't follow the conventions of this kind of teaching, but my results are just as good or better than the results of teachers who do. Of course, I think that has something to do with my twenty two years of experience!

So what about these nuggets of genius from the inspirational, experienced and naturally gifted teachers? I asked people for suggestions on how to create a dramatic, fun or unexpected lesson beginning. This is what people came up with:

- *The Magic Box*. Pupils put their hands into a box, containing an object/artefact related to the lesson. They have to describe it without looking and the rest of the class guess.
- *Interactive whiteboard*. Subject-related pictures projected on board, with a hidden message behind (like 'Catchphrase'), which pupils need to find.
- *Games involving key words*: such as anagrams, pictionary, odd-one-out, bingo, topic tennis, guess the question, making as many words as possible from one long word, hang-man, etc.

- *Photographs.* Pass round an image or selection of images, and use these to generate discussion.
- *Beat the teacher.* Each pupil has a (badly) written topic-related paragraph that they have to correct.

Read an example of work written by one of the pupils. Ask the class who wrote it. This appeals to their egocentricity.

Question catch. Quick fire questions, as a soft ball is thrown from the person asking the question to the person who answers it.

Getting another member of staff to role-play a conversation with you.

Little teachers. Give small groups of pupils some basic modelling materials (e.g. lolly-sticks, playdough, card) and 5 minutes to come up with a way of demonstrating an idea (e.g. soil erosion) to the rest of the class using the materials provided.

Silent beginning. Teachers and pupils try to communicate an idea or key word, using gesture/sign language.

One head teacher explains that although she values creative teaching and all the adventurous ways of drawing pupils into a lesson, there is still a need for routine and firm expectations:

I wouldn't expect my teachers to pull it out of the hat five times a day, five days a week. That would be far too tiring. There also needs to be some expectation on the part of the pupils – that they are there on time, sitting quietly and ready to start work, without having to be seduced into it.

This sentiment was echoed by other teachers who felt it was important to pace themselves, not only for their own sanity, but also because they felt that the mundane lessons gave more power to the special ones:

I go for my 'wow' lessons at the start of a new scheme of work . . . and then the motivation usually takes on a life of its own. If they seem to be flagging, I'll come up with something to refresh them; but I will also admit to my fair share of 'bin-work' (e.g. what I did in my holidays . . .) if I'm feeling tired or under pressure. It's about finding a balance.

Lessons benefit from variety. Ideally, a lesson would involve opportunities for listening, looking, speaking, moving and doing, encompassing all the different ways that people learn. However, it is also important that pupils have opportunities to be, at times, passively, as well as actively, involved with tasks. In other words, not everything needs to super-energised and practical. There needs to be down-time, not just to give the teacher a rest, but to allow for pupils to absorb and process everything that has been going on.

Reflection box:
How intense are you? Observe your teaching over the course of a week. Is it generally delivered at one pace, or do you have times where you give a lot and times where you pull back? If you find yourself slowing down at times, is it because you plan to, or because you've simply run out of energy?

Another important aspect of pace is the length of the lessons and how much time/how many different activities are incorporated into each session. The discussion group consensus was that longer lessons, of 1 hour to 90 minutes, are suitable for practical subjects, but opinions were mixed as to whether they are of benefit to other subjects. Some people felt that during longer lessons pupils started to fade halfway through, preferring bursts of 45–55 minutes. Others liked the fact that length gave them time to do more adventurous activities and to consolidate the learning.

Pupils certainly saw the benefit of doing several different activities during the course of a lesson, which helped sustain their interest, as long as they didn't feel they were being rushed, or not being given the opportunity to explore something properly. One primary school pupil explained:

I don't like it when the teachers tells us it's time to stop when I've been enjoying something and I haven't finished it. Some of my friends work quicker than me, so they get to finish all the work, but I don't.

Changes of activity or task can have a de-motivating effect if pupils feel they are constantly struggling to keep up and to get things finished within the allotted time. In a class where abilities are broad, it is inevitable that work rates will vary, making it a challenge for the teacher to pitch the level of difficulty and the timeframe of each task. Several pupils I talked to felt somewhat overlooked in this regard. They didn't necessarily make a fuss or get noticed for it. They seemed to be quietly fading, simply accepting they were not as able as their peers. For the 'perfect' teacher this will not do. Once again it comes down to knowing your pupils – perfect teaching is not simply a matter of applying the teacher-training college techniques (such as incorporating several different activities), but applying them with instinct and awareness of pupils' individual needs.

Here are some of the suggestion that were made on how lessons and activities can be broken down:

> Think of a lesson as having an introduction, two, three, sometimes four main tasks (for longer sessions), and then a plenary, plus time for getting ready and clearing up.
>
> Include a mix of teacher-led, group, pair and independent work.
>
> Spend the first 5/10 minutes on an easy starter, for example brainstorming or a spider diagram, to establish what they already know about the topic. Then they have something to build the rest of the lesson on.
>
> Break complex activities, such as essay writing, into manageable chunks (brainstorming, establishing key argument, organising points into paragraphs, introduction, conclusion).
>
> Model an example of the work you expect the pupils to do, so that they have a concrete starting point.
>
> Signify the end/beginning of different activities using interjections of music (e.g. the theme from 'Countdown'), or use timers: an alarm clock, kitchen timer or the interactive whiteboard feature, which will foster a sense of challenge to complete the work.
>
> Ask pupils to perform a mini-plenary before changing tasks, completing the sentences:
>
> One thing I have learned so far is . . .
>
> One thing I'm not sure about is . . .
>
> One question I'd like to ask is . . .

Be flexible: if something is going well/badly don't be afraid to
change the direction of the lesson. Sticking rigidly to the plan
can result in missed opportunities.

Have clearly established routines to organise the set up/clear up
and any movement around the class, which will minimise
time wasting.

Should the perfect teacher stick to her/his planned timeframe or
go with the pace of the pupils? It would not be good practice to
allow the pupils to demand or dictate the lesson direction, but it is
nevertheless wise to have a contingency for when you can see that
they are genuinely struggling to get something, or have finished
faster than you thought they would. I keep a folder of 'emergency'
extension activities, which can focus the more able students whilst
they are waiting for the rest of the class to catch up. And I pitch the
bulk of my teaching to the middle level, so I know there will
always be some who are faster and some who are slower.

On the issue of pace and timings one teacher argued:

It's not the pupils or the teachers that are the problem. It's that
the National Curriculum is too crowded. If the plan says move
on, I have to, regardless of whether most of the kids have got it
yet. The timeframe is too tight to dwell on one particular thing
for too long, otherwise chunks of the curriculum would be
missed out, which would be a risk for exam grades. This is not
how it should be, but it's how it is.

And an ex-head teacher provided a lovely metaphor to illustrate
this issue:

I would prefer an enriching meal of one thing, than a meagre
mouthful of lots of dishes or just being spoon-fed a few crumbs!

Indeed.

Key points for learning content, structure and pace:
> ➤ A variety of tasks can help keep lesson momentum going and
allow opportunities for pupils to engage with different skills,
but be aware of differing abilities.

> Try to provide opportunities for listening, looking, speaking, moving and doing.
> Think of the lesson as having different parts, involving teacher-led discussion, pair work and group work as well as individual work.
> Start with an explanation of the objectives but make sure that they are simple to digest and meaningful to the students (e.g. pose them as questions or short statements).
> Alternatively, create a dramatic or surprising lesson beginning that gets the class attention.
> For longer tasks, break them into chunks and build up in layers.
> To help pupils understand challenging ideas, try looking at the same point in a number of ways (e.g. through role-play, visual images, question and answer, formal explanation, model making).
> Develop a lesson structure that works for you, but don't be afraid to experiment occasionally. Keep it interesting for yourself, and your pupils.
> Be aware of pupils that are taking more time to complete work or take on ideas than others. If possible create some time during the week for 'finishing off'.
> Be prepared with extension activities for pupils who finish work quickly.

Assessment

Buzzwords in education come and go, and one of the recent ones is 'Assessment for Learning'. It is arguable that assessment has always been part of the teacher's responsibility, so this current emphasis is nothing too surprising, but like so many other new ideas and initiatives, it can sometimes seem like yet another pressure, along with all the Individual Education Plan (IEPs), Gifted and Talented, Every Child Matters, Personalised Learning, SATs, Speaking and Listening, Cross-curricular, Raising Standards and general 'Excellence' that is expected of us.

Assessment for Learning can be thought of as a journey, which explores the gap between where a learner is at, and where they need to get to. It helps you, and them, to decide and modify the direction that the learning activities take, in order to reach the final destination. To this purpose, it should inform what you teach and how you teach it. Effective assessment is an on-going, all-encompassing process – it's not just about marking a pile of books at the end of the week, which, in some ways, is merely checking that the learning has happened.

Although this may sound daunting, in actual fact, teachers have been doing it informally, and sometimes formally, for years. It has always seemed logical to me that pupils have targets to work towards, follow small steps to get to the big idea, and are regularly questioned and given feedback so that they, and I, are clear about their progress.

The 'perfect' teacher, it seems, is able to use assessment as a teaching 'tool', rather than something that is done to oblige the Head of Department. So how do they do this without working themselves into the ground? The trick is to separate the core, useful aspects of assessment, and recognise how they can support and improve your classroom work, from the jargon. When asked what they felt the key purpose of assessment was, one primary teacher said:

> It has got to be useful. It can be useful to a number of people: to you, helping you to recognise what knowledge your pupils do and don't have; to your pupils, helping them to discover their strengths and weaknesses; and to parents, who like to know what their children are capable of – but ultimately it has *got* to be useful . . . otherwise it's just paper shovelling.

However, usefulness to one group of people is not always usefulness to another; therefore, tensions can arise. A Further Education lecturer described one of these tensions:

> My concern is that the learning now has to be so structured, that there isn't enough time for actual teaching. They (the students) are working through a checklist, having to prove that they've covered points a), b) and c), but without the time to explore their understanding. Constantly having to check where your students are at is taking a lot of time away from teaching.

This point echoed the sentiments of many, including parents, who expressed concern that, with such heavy emphasis on targets and attainment, there is too little time left in the curriculum for pupils to explore and question what they are being taught. Some teachers explained that they had had to turn to more traditional, didactic teaching methods such as learning by rote, in order that pupils were prepared for their exams: teaching bare facts rather than teaching critical thinking. Assessment therefore becomes trapped in the drive for results. An experienced teacher and teacher-training lecturer lamented the issue:

> The best kind of assessment is intuitive. The 'perfect' teacher does it on their feet. It's about knowing and understanding the individual pupils in your class. It's a skill that you learn over time. Unfortunately this skill has been taken over and made into something unnatural: standardised tests. People make the mistake of thinking that good assessment is about nice neat files and lists of children's names; that teaching can be measured by standards. But it can't and it just puts pressure on staff, who start believing that the amount of paperwork they have relates to the effectiveness of their teaching.

On hearing this point of view, a parent governor raised a counter concern:

> It would be naïve of us to think that every single teacher is one of those amazing, intuitive, 'natural' ones. Great though they are, they are few and far between. The majority are sound but middle-of-the-road, and a structured approach to assessment could help them to relate to their pupils' learning better, as long as it isn't so over complicated that it becomes unmanageable.

Reflection box:
What is the purpose of assessment in your class/department? In what way does it benefit you? Your pupils?

I asked school inspectors what they were looking for in terms of assessment. These are the key suggestions:

- Assessment is used to inform future planning. Knowing where your pupils are at enables you to set more meaningful tasks and ensure that key concepts and themes are not being missed out.

- A variety of methods are used, some intuitive (based on your knowledge of your pupils, your subject and your experience), some informal (question and answer sessions, general response of pupils to a task or lesson, discussion about work, peer assessments) and some formal (written tests, oral tests, timed essays, presentations).
- Regular feedback to students (one-to-one discussions, noting common errors, setting individual/whole-class targets, oral feedback to class).
- Statements about pupils work that are specific, and that, where possible, are followed up (e.g. 'You have correctly used a variety of interesting adjectives which brings your writing to life', rather than 'good work', and that further progress in this area is monitored, 'Your use of adjectives continues to improve – well done! Try using a thesaurus for further ideas.').
- A culture of reflective learning that is built into the lesson. Allow a brief amount of time for the class to look back over their work, and discuss any strengths/areas for improvement, which gives more value to the assessments the teacher makes.
- Recognise the need for accountability, and marry the useful, intuitive stuff with keeping clear records, which may well prove useful to you in the end (e.g. at parent's evenings).
- Have a realistic approach that doesn't over-burden you. Assess in groups – focus on a few pupil at the top, a few at the bottom, a general 'best fit' for the whole-class, and one or two that need extra support.

For parents, it seems the rigorousness of standardised testing can be a useful thing. One parent commented:

We need to know what's happening in our children's learning. We don't always have an in-depth understanding of the curriculum, so it is helpful to be able to draw a quick comparison between our child's results and other children in the year group. It gives us a benchmark. It is also reassuring to think that the majority of teachers are working from the same page. There is, or should be, some consistency about what is being taught and what experiences children have.

However, on the other side of the fence, the opposite can sometimes occur. Some teachers raised concern about the lack of consistency that arises from assessment and, specifically, attainment targets:

> Teachers don't always have faith in other teachers' assessments, so they waste time redoing them again. It is particularly bad across key stages. Sometimes I look at the Levels my pupils have been given and I can't believe that their previous teacher knew them at all! It is misleading to everyone, including the pupils.

Of course, the 'perfect' teacher would never make a mistake like that! Perhaps this issue highlights the value of assessing within a team, working alongside your colleagues to ensure that your own interpretation of a pupil's ability is shared by others. It also brings us back to the idea of effective assessment as being intuitive, and based on experience. Accurate assessment is not something that inexperienced (and sometimes experienced) teachers are naturally accustomed to. It takes time to establish an understanding of the curriculum, the differences between pupils and the nature of learning. Being able to dissect and evaluate these things is a skill in itself.

Key points for assessment:
- Progression and assessment are closely linked: use your assessment to inform your planning.
- Good teachers give specific feedback. 'Perfect' teachers follow up on it.
- Use a variety of different methods, formal and informal.
- Incorporate a brief amount of reflective time into lessons, to look over previously assessed work with pupils, which helps to keep them, and you, in touch with it.
- Avoid burnout by developing an effective but 'realistic' approach: have a 'best fit' for the whole-class, and then focus

more carefully on a few individuals. Choose different individuals each term/half a term.

> Assessment can take time to become accustomed to, so seek guidance from colleagues and mentors, and make the most of opportunities to assess work alongside members of your department or year group.

> Marry your intuitive skill with your responsibility to be accountable for the learning that goes on in your classroom. And remember that paperwork can be useful: records of test results and homework can stop a pushy parent in their tracks!

Pupil motivation

The issue of pupil motivation presents a number of challenges, which largely stem from the nature and ability of the pupils in the class. How do we make learning exciting, meaningful, useful, enjoyable and achievement-orientated to each individual pupil, given the varied make-up of our class groups? At the top end, we may have keen, bright young things who want to be stretched and challenged and given work that even the teacher doesn't understand. At the bottom, we have the reluctant tribe: the truants and the rebels, who have lost their appetite for learning, yet are perhaps not without potential. And then, of course, there is every variation in-between.

One member of my discussion group felt that the answer was straightforward:

If a lesson is well prepared and delivered, and the teacher spurs pupils onwards, giving them frequent encouragement and feedback, then this, in itself, is motivating.

Goodness, you're probably saying . . . if only it really was that simple! Although it is at least a good place to start. A secondary school pupil from London explained:

I like Geography lessons the most, because the teacher explains things properly and makes it interesting. If you don't understand something, he helps you and he doesn't get annoyed about it.

I used to like French as well, but our new teacher is really boring, and just makes you copy things out. The other French class
are always going to the library or the ICT room. I think they are
having more fun. Some of my friends are deliberately trying to
do badly with their grades, so that they can get moved down
into that class.

Enlightening stuff.

Other people shared different stories of the struggles they faced
getting pupils motivated to learn, and it often led towards reflection on *why* this is the case:

I think it happens in the home and the wider community.
Sometimes I feel like I'm fighting a losing battle against the lure
of gossip, junk culture and television. I spend hours preparing
lovely, interesting tasks that I think my Year 6s will really enjoy,
and then all they want to do is socialise or wind each other up.
They don't see the value of education, because we're the only
ones telling them it has any value – and why should they listen
to us? We're the enemy.

One Deputy Head, based in an inner city secondary school, had
an even bleaker perspective:

I see a lot of chronic disaffection: pupils who are reluctant to set
foot in school, let alone engage with any kind of learning process. They don't recognise the school environment as something
for them, because historically it has not been a positive part of
their experience. Education may not matter within their families, or reflect their plans for the future. The majority of pupils
can, with effort, be clawed back into the fold, but there is always
that percentage that is too far away to be reached. Sadly, I think
the number of these kind of students is on the increase.

Reflection box:
How motivated are your pupils to learn and participate in
lessons? What are the factors that affect their motivation? How
much influence do you feel you can have on these factors?

Suggestions as to how the 'perfect' teacher could endeavour to motivate pupils were plentiful. All of these, according to their claimants, are tried and tested and proven to have results:

- Biscuits! Given to pupils from all year groups who have a completed merit chart.
- If a child knows that her/his teacher is always ready to listen to her/him whatever the issue, problem or question, she/he will usually do anything for them.
- A cheerful smile and a sense of humour.
- Favourite activities, such as ICT or games, used as either part of the lesson or as reward for completing work.
- Simple, quick rewards: stickers, stamps, sweets, note home, small jobs, marbles.
- Always explaining to pupils what they will be learning in the next topic – getting them to research and prepare questions ahead of the event, so that their enthusiasm is already ignited.
- Explaining activities and generating interest at the beginning of the day/lesson so that they do not start the day thinking it is one 'boring' thing after another.
- Explaining to pupils *why* they are learning what they are, and how it will help them.
- Incorporating pupils' own ideas into the progression of the lesson.
- Praising small achievements, such as handing in homework on time, or neat work, particularly for low-ability pupils.
- Displaying the work of pupils of all abilities.
- Getting pupils to work in 'teams' to earn points or prizes for good behaviour or work. Peer pressure encourages them to cooperate.
- Breaking big tasks into 'chunks' so that students are supported through work that might otherwise seem overwhelming.
- Giving pupils responsibilities: taking the register, giving out equipment, writing on the board or even taking part of the lesson.
- Finding the core of the lesson that may be interesting or relevant to the pupils and emphasising this, for example

themes such as 'falling in love', 'being in trouble' or things that are shocking to them and get a personal response.

- Honesty: 'I want you to achieve and I know you can do better.'
- Personal attention and getting to know them, making them feel valued as individuals and welcomed into your class.
- Music, either soothing to calm them down, or played quietly as a reward for good behaviour.

Some individuals felt very strongly that 'perfect' teachers should not have to go down the bribery route:

Anyone can hand out a bag of sweets, give a fleeting smile and say 'well done', but the real gift is looking into a child's eyes and sincerely explaining what they have done to deserve your praise and attention. The only genuine way to motivate a class is to be calm and consistent, and to create an atmosphere of appreciation, giving carefully considered praise and personal attention when warranted. This works for students of all ages.

Within the discussion group, it seemed that less experienced teachers were more likely to make use of extrinsic motivators (such as points charts and tangible rewards), whereas more experienced staff backed the viewpoint that these things can be overused. One secondary school teacher even felt that praise was being used to excess:

Too many teachers constantly and continuously seem to praise pupils for behaviour which our society actually expects as the norm. They make a big deal over things that should simply be intrinsically in place (for example, arriving on time, using manners).

Reflection box:
How do you use praise and how frequently do you use it? Pay attention to your interactions with your pupils over the course of a lesson. Are your comments having a positive effect? Are you using them too much, or without meaning, or too little?

For some, the idea of using tangible rewards ('bribes') to motivate pupils is unacceptable. This perspective was expressed by a
parent, who was concerned that her own children were missing
out simply because they were not the ones that causing problems:

> I am disgusted that the government is offering cash to students
> to motivate them to turn up to school. Lazy students get rewards
> whilst the hard working ones are ignored. What can be more
> de-motivating than seeing the student that has constantly
> mucked around and disrupted your lesson being given a wad of
> cash and a pat on the back for sitting still for five minutes. What's
> wrong with simply getting good grades?

However, a youth and community worker raised the concern
that motivation is closely connected to an individual's self-esteem,
and that many of the most challenging and reluctant learners are
also the most vulnerable:

> It always seems as if those who need the most motivation get the
> least rewards . . . these kids often don't get the experiences and
> opportunities that a lot of other kids get, and they definitely
> don't get support and encouragement from their parents. At
> school, we (the staff) are the ones that actually do take an inter-
> est. Sometimes it's a case of building up their self-esteem from
> the most basic level, through saying 'well done, you turned up
> today . . .' The most effective teachers I work with know how
> to boost their pupils with continuous little incentives. These
> kids don't have the internal desire to do it for themselves, so
> they need constant reinforcement.

Certainly, from my own experience, working with extremely
challenging and disaffected teenagers, there was always a need to
use obvious quick-fix external motivators, such as sticker charts and
prizes, as a starting point. These individuals had very little capacity
for motivating themselves, so if we were to get anywhere initially,
it required tangible incentives. Many of them could not cope with
praise. They lacked self-esteem, and were highly anxious about
engaging with the processes of the classroom environment – which
would often translate as aggression, silliness or refusal to cooperate.

In the first instance, I would set up very clear opportunities for tangible reward, and once they were comfortable with that, I would start to work on their inner pride. But it was a long process.

The way to address pupil motivation (or lack of) is clearly not a straightforward one, and is dependent, not just on the individual pupils, but on the wider issues and influences of social culture. Even the most 'perfect' of teachers, therefore, has her/his work cut out for her/him, and will have to take into account the individual needs of her/his students when considering how best to engage their enthusiasm. One thing is absolutely clear – success begins with 'knowing' the pupils that you are working with.

Key points for pupil motivation:
> Don't get too caught up in tangible rewards. They may work in the short term, but will eventually lose effectiveness. They can, however, provide a useful starting point for very reluctant groups.
> Use praise, as long as it is meaningful and sincere, and is genuinely merited.
> Recognise that in some class groups, pupils will have very different experiences of intrinsic (internal) motivation, and that you may have to modify your approach according to the needs of individuals.
> Be positive and welcoming. A warm smile goes a long way, for little effort.
> Provide clear expectations about forthcoming activities, and get pupils thinking about topics in advance.
> Try to see learning activities from your pupils' point of view: what would make them more interesting? More challenging? More manageable? More relevant?
> Convey a sense of real interest in you pupils. Acknowledge effort and achievement with your time, attention and personal interest.

Special educational needs (SEN) and differentiation

Teaching pupils with SEN can be extremely rewarding, but it is also a source of anxiety for many teachers, who may feel they do not have the necessary experience, knowledge or insights to take on this role effectively. A mainstream primary class teacher explains:

> Last year I had two Autistic pupils in my class, as well as a number of pupils with behaviour and learning difficulties. This is not unusual in my school – it seems to be the norm. I enjoy my job, but it's so hard to keep everything in check, and I don't feel like I've been trained for this.

As an experienced special needs teacher myself, I would say one of the most important things you can do to successfully support SEN pupils in your classroom, is to get to know them. Gather all the information you can about their needs, their level of ability, and any medical/health issues (if necessary, communicate with the special needs coordinator and/or teaching assistants who should be able to guide you, and make sure you are aware of relevant documentation IEPs, behaviour plans, statements), but also take the time to build a personal relationship with the pupil. Find out what motivates them, what they respond to, what they like and dislike. It is this sort of knowledge that will truly enable you to get through barriers and better understand how you can support their learning.

Reflection box:
Think of an SEN pupil you have worked with. How much prior information did you have about the pupil and her/his needs before you met the pupil? How did this affect your relationship with her/him?

'SEN' is an umbrella term that needs to be broken down in order to have relevance to individual pupils. One child's needs may be wildly different from another's. Definitions come and go, but we can broadly categorise different types of needs as follows:

- Cognition and learning (e.g. dyslexia, dyspraxia or developmental delay)
- Communication and interaction (e.g. Autistic Spectrum Conditions, such as Asperger's Syndrome)

- Social, emotional and behavioural development (such as conduct disorders, or Attention Deficit and Hyperactivity Disorders)
- Sensory and/or physical (e.g. hearing and visual impairments, muscular dystrophy).

It is possible that pupils will have more than one need to contend with, and issues in one area can often impact on another. I have worked with a number of students who are defined not only as having 'social, emotional and behavioural difficulties', but also as having learning difficulties; and likewise, students with 'communication' difficulties who also have behavioural problems, often attributable to the frustration they experience in not being able to get their point across.

Levels of need can vary considerably. It is likely that pupils with the most challenging level of need (such as those with severe (SLD) or profound and multiple (PMLD) difficulties) will be catered for in special schools, where they will have access to resources, facilities and specially trained staff. However, the on-going focus on 'inclusion', means that SEN pupils are, where possible, being educated within the mainstream setting, particularly those with mild to moderate levels of need.

So what implications does this have for the mainstream class teacher? A special needs coordinator in my discussion group commented:

> Part of my role involves making sure that SEN pupils are not undervalued – that they are given as much opportunity to fulfil their potential as any other pupil in the school. I do what I can to support teachers, whether that's providing resources, classroom support, or information . . . but ultimately, there are those who embrace the inclusion of SEN pupils in their class, and there are those who simply don't want to know.

Reflection box:
What has been your experience of working with pupils with SEN? Do you see 'inclusion' is a positive thing, or just special-education-on-the-cheap? Are there any benefits, for both the SEN pupils themselves, and for their mainstream peers?

Whatever our personal views on inclusion are, if you are required to teach pupils with SEN then there are a number of things you will need to take account of in your teaching, which brings us to the question of 'differentiation'.

> Do you know what level of ability the pupils have, or how their needs may affect their participation in certain activities? (Take care not to over- or underestimate, and if in doubt, ask your special needs team and/or other staff for some guidance. Remember that physical disabilities do not automatically mean pupils will have impaired cognitive ability).
>
> Are you taking account of these issues when setting work? (Be mindful of physical disabilities they may affect a child's ability to participate, or visual/hearing impairments e.g. if the class are looking at images, can a sensory alternative, for example, a smell or taste, be provided for a pupil who has limited vision.)
>
> As appropriate, are you providing suitable learning aids (e.g. word lists, individual targets) and differentiated resources (e.g. simplified worksheets, sensory resources)?
>
> Are you ensuring that the pupil feels included within the class/ group? (Be careful not to isolate or draw attention to their differences, and understand that SEN pupils may have friends or groups of people they prefer working/playing with.)
>
> Have you adapted your expectations accordingly? (SEN pupils need to be stretched and given challenges, like any other pupil – but these challenges need to be realistic and achievable. You may have to break targets down into bite-sized steps, in order to track progress and make things meaningful to the pupil.)

The issue of differentiation raised some debate within my discussion group. Getting it right can have a number of benefits: pupils will have more motivation if they feel the learning opportunities are appealing and within their grasp, which will lead to more on-task behaviour, which will, in turn, reduce disruptive behaviour and attitude. But even the most perfect of perfect teachers may struggle with this at times. As one secondary teacher suggested:

We are supposed to find ways of including everybody, and personalising the learning . . . but if I was to do that for every pupil in every lesson, I would wear myself out in a matter of weeks. Unfortunately, I find myself tending to rely on differentiation by outcome – most of the kids achieve some of the objectives and some of them achieve all. It's not ideal, but I just don't have enough time. What am I supposed to do?

The alternative to the 'mixed-ability class' is the class or year group that is 'streamed'. Concerns about this were mentioned a number of times. Some felt that the use of banding or setting pupils according to ability is a negative thing. A learning mentor explained:

> It simply reinforces the view that some children are 'clever' and some are 'thick' – this can be very stigmatising. I always explain to pupils that intelligence and ability comes in many different forms, and that academic results are just a small part of your achievements.

And a number of teachers raised concerns about the impact that streaming has on behaviour:

> The low ability sets are often the ones feared by teachers, because of the high volume of poor behaviour that goes on. Personally, I find the high-ability groups to be my most challenging behaviour-wise. They are often very arrogant, rude and full of attitude. Add to this the fact that all groups are a mix to some degree – all those middle sets that are neither here nor there.

If you are contending with a class (or classes) of pupils where the variation in ability is broad, make sure you have realistic expectations of yourself and what you can achieve. It may be a case of simplifying your planning so that it takes account of two or three general levels of ability, with some special attention to the most needy individuals – a 'best fit' approach.

Also look at how you can best utilise the space of the classroom, and, crucially, any additional staff (learning mentors, teaching assistants, etc.) that may be present. If they are confident and competent (see section on Working with teaching assistants), they may be happy leading a group of pupils themselves in one area of the classroom, whilst you can lead another group, and possibly a further group can work independently; before all joining back together at the end of the lesson to review what has been learned.

Key points for SEN and differentiation:

> Building a relationship with an SEN pupil will help you to get to know and understand her/his learning needs – look for the personality before the need itself.

> Ensure that you have familiarised yourself with any necessary documentation relating to that pupil, and if in doubt, speak to your school's special needs staff.

> Special needs can relate to different aspects of person's development (e.g. cognitive, communication, behaviour, physical), and these have very different consequences.

> Think of a pupil's special needs as challenges to overcome rather than barriers or problems – sometimes this requires a bit of creative or lateral thinking.

> Effective differentiation depends on understanding the pupil's level of ability – use this as your starting point, and if you are not sure, carry out some assessments activities.

> Make sure you adjust your pupil expectations accordingly – SEN pupils may progress in much smaller steps.

> Have a realistic expectation of yourself, and look out how you can maximise your resources (e.g. staff, space, equipment) to make the process of differentiation easier.

3 Dealing with discipline

Creating calm

A calm classroom is a pleasant place to be. Everyone goes about their business thoughtfully and respectfully. Voices are rarely raised. Pupils are settled and focused on their learning – they know what is expected of them. And the teacher is able to teach, without interruptions, and with positive enthusiasm. There is no doubt that a calm, stable atmosphere is beneficial to all who work in it. In contrast, an environment, where noise, shouting, fraying tempers and constant interruptions are commonplace, conjures up images of frazzled teachers and disengaged pupils, and stress for everyone.

So how does one establish an oasis of tranquillity within their classroom? Perhaps it is the osmosis effect, as one parent recalls:

> My child's best teacher was a quiet lady who must have been in her late fifties. To look at her, you wouldn't have thought she would have any impact on the class, but there were never any problems in her lessons. All of the children respected her, and paid attention to whatever she said. She never shouted, and in fact, she spoke very softly. She was so calm with them, that they couldn't help being calm around her.

Having your own sense of personal calm is a good place to start. That's not to suggest that it is an easy thing to do, given the many stresses and pressures that teachers face throughout the day. I asked a number of teachers what wound them up at school. Common aggravations were as follows:

- Not being listened to by pupils
- Pupils disrespecting or damaging resources

- Lack of resources
- Pupils being rude to you
- Pupils bullying one another
- Pupils expecting you to do the work for them
- Being undermined by other members of staff
- Lack of support from senior management
- Inconsistency
- Paperwork
- Lack of time

Interestingly, several of these issues were not that different from the responses I received when asking what winds pupils up at school, which included not being listened to, being told what to do, inconsistency, bullying, and teachers being rude to them.

Reflection box:
What presses your buttons? What presses your pupils buttons? Are there any similarities?

Everyone feels frustration, stress and anger. They are perfectly rational emotional responses to difficult situations. The key is in how these emotional responses are managed and expressed. Whilst we cannot necessarily control the way our pupils react to the things that wind them up (which could include anything from excitable silliness to aggressive assault), we can, hopefully, control the way we respond to our own anger and stress. And in so doing, we can maintain a personal sense of calm and use this, in turn, to help calm our pupils down.

I asked staff how they managed to remain calm under pressure and although everyone acknowledged that, at times, it was almost impossible, there were many helpful suggestions:

Counting to ten
Focusing on breathing out slowly (rather than breathing in, which can cause hyperventilation and make you feel more stressed)
Moving away from pupils that are trying to entangle you into an argument

Being business like and matter-of-fact with difficult pupils,
    rather than emotional

Telling yourself its just a job

Telling yourself that its not personal, and that the pupils have
    their own problems

Drinking plenty of water

Stopping the lesson and getting everyone to put their heads
    down and be silent for a couple of minutes

Knowing that you can offload in the staff-room

Giving pupils take-up time, that is giving them an instruction
    and then moving away

Working with groups or individuals who *do* want to take part in
    the lesson

Thinking about plans for the weekend

Deferring your response, that is 'I'll speak to you at the end of
    the lesson.'

Being able to maintain a sense of controlled calm under pressure
allows you to react to problems in the classroom through your
skill, rather than through your emotion. As one senior teacher
warns:

> The classic is when a member of staff overreacts to something
> fairly minor; for example, if a child loses concentration and starts
> chatting to their mate, then all of a sudden the teacher confronts
> them with a barrage of ranting. Running out of patience and
> having a go at pupils is NOT a behaviour management strategy.
> It is desperation.

This is a notion I whole-heartedly agree with. Effective, calm
classroom management is about responding to situations with skill
and professionalism, rather than uncontrolled, reactive emotion.
That is not to say that emotions cannot be expressed, or indeed, be
effective in making pupils recognise how their behaviour affects
you, but that these emotions need to be well judged. In Chapter 1,
You and your teaching style, several references were made to the
idea that teaching is akin to acting, a performance of sorts. The
tactical handling of emotion within the classroom is a good example of this: a judicious display of disappointment can trigger solemn

regret from an irresponsible pupil; an artful expression of shock can convince her/him that you truly expected better.

But untamed, reactionary outbursts of anger, irritation or impatience, can easily have the opposite effect. The danger of allowing such emotions to dictate your teaching and classroom management is that you may appear to your pupils as someone who is unpredictable or erratic. At its least, this will be a cue for some pupils to get a kick out of winding you up; and at its worst, will make pupils feel anxious and threatened. Neither result is conducive to a positive atmosphere for learning.

There is, of course, that percentage of teachers who use anger as a method of pupil control on a daily basis, and to powerful effect; but it is tricky to pull this one off, and still have the respect of the pupils. It is also tricky to pull it off if you can't convince utterly. A teacher-training lecturer made this observation:

> A lot of new teachers can be confused by what they believe to be effective behaviour management. They see these big forceful characters throwing their weight around, and think that that is the way to do it. They try to be strict and scary and are disappointed when it doesn't have any effect, or they just get laughed at.

The fact is, that 'don't mess with me' teacher presence takes time to cultivate. It relies on establishing a fearsome reputation and, at the risk of sounding old-fashioned, often has something to do with having a certain 'look': for instance, an intimidating physical stature, or a particularly loud voice. And rest assured, the angry approach is not always the best way – it can easily be tantamount to bullying. I reassure new and experienced teachers alike that being calm, fair and consistent will enable you to establish good classroom control *and* give you a better relationship with your students in the long term.

Beyond being a self-aware oasis if calm yourself, other suggestions for how to foster a calm classroom atmosphere are as follows:

- Establish routines for busy transition times, such as entering the classroom or tidying up (see Chapter 4 on Organising the classroom).
- Have an orderly beginning and end to lessons.

- Have clear, consistent expectations that pupils are familiar with.
- Have engaging and easily accessed starter activities that will focus the pupils as soon as they enter the classroom (e.g. a word or picture puzzle on the board).
- With more challenging groups, be prepared to spend some time focusing on behaviour expectations and classroom routines, before trying to push ahead with the curriculum.
- Be aware of the difference between 'shouting' and 'raising your voice', and remember that the former is never helpful and the latter is only helpful if it is used sparingly.
- Don't attempt to do too much too quickly straight after break, lunch or PE – allow for some settling down time.
- If necessary, allow pupils to get a drink (of water). Dehydration can make people irritable and easily distracted.
- Use kinaesthetic games/songs (e.g. Braingym) to create group cohesion and to work off excess energy.
- If possible, consider the timetable: activities that are more 'hands-on' can be effective during restless afternoon sessions.
- Play quiet, calming music.
- Hold up visual cues (e.g. a card with a picture of someone with their finger to their lips) to encourage pupils to keep the noise level down.

The last suggestion was taken from an idea given to me by a SENCO, who found that visual cue cards, featuring cartoon faces expressing a variety of different emotions, was helpful in maintaining a stable classroom atmosphere and managing low-level disruptions. Importantly, it also encouraged pupils to be aware of the effects of their actions and to be more sensitive to different emotions:

If there was something going on, I would quietly hold up a particular picture card, featuring cartoon pictures of teachers. There were several: sad teacher, shocked teacher, happy teacher, tired teacher, worried teacher, cross teacher, and so on. Once the pupils had noticed the card, it was their responsibility to suggest what the picture meant I was feeling and why. It was extremely effective in getting them to reflect and modify their actions, without me having to say a word. Gradually they became much more empathic, not just towards me, but towards each other as well.

Of course, the success of a strategy such as this relies on having a positive relationship with the class in the first place. They need to want to cooperate with you, and to have your respect, in order to not want to upset or disturb you. Ultimately, everything in the 'perfect' teachers toolbox links together: relating positively and respectfully to your pupils helps to create a calm, pleasant classroom atmosphere, which in turn makes it easier to build upon that positive relationship.

Key points for creating calm:
> Understand your own triggers of stress and frustration and find ways of letting off steam away from the classroom
> Deal with difficulties in a low-level way where possible (see section on Whole-class low-level disruption).
> Model calm behaviour yourself. If you are calm, it is likely that this will help your pupils to feel calm.
> React to problems with your professional skill rather than knee-jerk emotions.
> Save raising your voice for occasional use and for purposeful effect.
> Recognise that some lessons are going to be more challenging than others (e.g. straight after break, afternoons, last lesson on a Friday).
> Don't put pressure on yourself by having unrealistic expectations of what you can achieve in these times, and where possible, consider adapting the timetable/activities (a lot of teachers seem to swear by sewing and knitting as a calming classroom activity!).

Whole-class low-level disruption

Another key factor in establishing calm is ensuring that the dreaded low-level behaviour problems are addressed. Easier said than done, because judging by discussions with teachers up and down the country, low-level disruption is the bane of their teaching lives; and frequently the problems are not just confined to one or two individuals, but can be the handy work of large groups or even whole classes of students. The kinds of behaviours teachers are experiencing (even the 'perfect' ones) include the following:

Calling out across the classroom
Persistently talking over the teacher
Getting out of seats at inappropriate times
Silly, attention-seeking noises
Lack of basic courtesy
Too much collective classroom noise
Cheeky or impertinent remarks
Hindering other students
Fidgeting and restless behaviours
Giving inappropriate responses to teacher questions
Non-directed swearing (i.e. not *at* anybody)
Verbal banter
Infringement of basic school rules (e.g. chewing gum, uniform, mobile phones, etc.)
Avoiding starting work
Mucking around with equipment
Lack of personal organisation and equipment
Arriving late
Laziness
Lack of engagement or enthusiasm

Does all of this sound painfully familiar? Perhaps the nub of this issue is not the behaviour itself, but the frequency with which it occurs: the *persistence*. Tormented from Manchester explains:

I am driven mad by the constant interruptions. With certain classes it is a virtual impossibility to even start the lesson. By the time most of them have arrived and got their coats off, and their pens ready (if they bother to bring them), we've lost ten minutes. To then get them quiet and focused on me is another ten minutes, by which point, some of the brighter ones have got bored and start mucking around. From then on, it's a constant battle of waiting for silence, finally getting it, uttering my first few words, and then the chatter starting up again – it seems like every time I open my mouth to speak, they open theirs.

And then of course, there are the late comers, who saunter in and disrupt everyone.

Arrgghhh! Half the lesson wasted, one frustration after another, and all the while, you are conscious of the fact that exams are on the horizon, the coursework deadline is imminent, and there are acres of curriculum still to get through. Not to mention the wasted hours spent preparing resources and activities that never get done. Pressure. Frustration. And demoralisation. Does it always have to be like this?

My advice in the first instance would be to take a step back. Have a long, relaxing sit down and, should you so desire, a stiff drink! Take comfort in the fact that if you are experiencing difficult lesson beginnings and persistent disruptions such as the above, you are not alone. Second, reassure yourself that reclaiming your lesson from the mob is not impossible – hard work, but not impossible.

Reflection box:
What do you think the triggers of low-level disruption in your classroom are? To what extent can you remove or deal with these triggers?

As with any behaviour issue, the starting point should always be a reflection on *why* problems are occurring: the triggers. Understanding, or at least having an idea, of what these triggers are gives you something to go on. It enables your interventions to be more purposeful and focused, and thereby more likely to achieve results. Of course, this can sometimes mean asking and answering some difficult questions about your own teaching and behaviour management style. Common triggers include the following:

- *Whole-school issues*: behaviour management policy not successfully established and maintained, inconsistency amongst staff, lack of support between staff, weak leadership, high staff turnover and lack of stability, demoralised or depressed culture amongst school (no point in trying).
- *Subject-related issues*: genuine boredom (work too hard or too easy), perceived boredom (assumptions that task or lesson

will be dull, pointless, etc. – some subjects struggle with this more than others), anxieties about ability, teachers own lack of understanding or motivation for the subject.

- *Pupil expectations of the teacher*: assumption that behaviour will not be dealt with (think they can get away with it – especially if they have been able to in the past), desire to challenge you if you are new or inexperienced, assumption that you will be easy (and fun) to wind up, desire to challenge you if they perceive you to be unreasonable or unfair.

- *Teacher approach*: lacking the confidence to stamp your mark, giving off signals that you resent the pupils/don't care about them/don't want them in your classroom, inconsistency of response, taking things personally, getting caught up in arguments and power struggles, letting too many things go.

- *Pupil attitude*: disengagement (idea that school is for socialising, not learning), competition between disruptive students (who is the ringleader?), competition between pupils and teacher (both wanting to be in control), lack of value placed on academic progress, indifference to rules and consequences, perception that they are the 'naughty' 'problem' class (living up to the label).

This list is by no means exhaustive, but maybe something strikes a chord with you. If it does, then what can you do about it? First, it is important to recognise that some triggers of challenging behaviour are within your control, and some are unfortunately beyond it. A behaviour support teacher from London highlighted this point:

> One of the biggest frustrations of the job is that, everyday, when the final bell goes, I know that my pupils will leave behind all the support and structure I have painstakingly provided for them in school, and will go back to their erratic home and social lives, have arguments with their families, drink alcohol on the streets, and all my efforts will be unravelled.

Some factors are just too big, and too farreaching, for the humble teacher to fully deal with. It is what we may strive towards, but ultimately, we do not have the capacity to just click our fingers and transform society. As for whole-school issues, which I'm sure produced many a sigh and roll of the eyes, from my experience, it seems that, for all the teachers who feel they are at the mercy of unsupportive, weak management teams and/or staff who constantly undermine one another; there are just as many, who talk about fantastic support, effective policies and successful teamwork. The good schools are clearly out there, but unfortunately they can't accommodate everyone.

If you are struggling in a chaotic and/or unsupportive school, it may be up to you to create your own personal sanctuary of peace within your classroom; and to seek out like-minded staff members who will support you and help form a team. If you are teaching a subject that is deemed unpopular by your students, you will need to think creatively about how to make the subject relevant and attractive to them (see Chapter 2, section on Lesson content and pace). If you are battling with pupil assumptions about who you are and what you are about, then recognise that you are in a strong position: the chances are they are testing you and looking to see where you draw the boundaries – they are, at least, interested in the effect you are going to have. If, however, your problem is student apathy and disengagement, you may face an on-going mission to raise their self-esteem and encourage them to identify with the values of good education, good social skills, good self-control, etc. – lots of encouragement, lots of modelling desired behaviour, lots of patience, lots of empathy, lots of time and lots of attention. And lastly, if you have the courage to recognise that *you* may be the one causing the problem, then you have this book to steer you on the right pathway!

Reflection box:
What effect does your reaction to your pupils' behaviour have? Do they take you seriously? Do they get angry with you? Do they answer back? Do they smirk and act unbothered? What effect would you like it to have?

So now, on a more strategic level, here are the golden rules for tackling whole-class low-level disruption:

Persistency and consistency: the number one rule – to have an impact on behaviour you need to be prepared to dig your heals in and stay the distance. If you diligently pick up on any little infringement of your expectations, and allow desired classroom behaviour to be your focus for a few weeks, you will eventually see results. If, on the other hand, you are casual and inconsistent in your attention to problems, your pupils may not take you seriously.

Use a sliding scale of interventions: low-level behaviours require low-level responses. Wherever possible, talk personally to the pupil(s) involved (i.e. know their names, avoid shouting across the room); express shock or surprise that they have gone against your expectations, but not anger; keep your voice quiet and calm, and project assertiveness. Avoid over-talking a problem – simply make your expectations clear and emphasise what you want them to do, rather than what you don't. If you have started low-level, than you will have some-where to go next, should the behaviour continue or become more serious (see sections on Rewards and sanctions, and Establishing boundaries).

Shake things up: with extremely difficult groups, your biggest challenge may be simply getting through to them in the first place. In this instance, and I have done this myself, it is help-ful to call in the support of a partner – another member of staff with a strong behaviour management record, who can use their presence to help establish a level of calm, allowing you to start making some inroads and lay the foundations of your expectations. Alternatively, it can be useful to focus your energy into one or two key expectations, and just work hard at getting pupils to follow these (e.g. listening when the teacher is talking) – once they are in the habit of respecting one expectation, they will be more accepting of others.

Work on the preventative: certain 'tricks' can help to reduce the likelihood of low-level behaviours becoming chronic, such as lesson starters to focus pupils when they come in (tasks that are fun, simple and 'do-ey': puzzles, anagrams, crosswords, etc.), clear routines, visual cues to help manage the classroom (red/yellow cards for warning pupils about behaviour, timers, writing names on board), praise, quick rewards for good behaviour (such as merits, stickers, stamps, comments in plan-ner, or a note home) – sometimes an element of competition can be effective (e.g. between different tables or groups).

Manage the entrance: if lesson beginnings are the problem, look at how pupils come into the class. Are they already there when you arrive? Do they bundle into the classroom as they please? If your first contact with them is not calm and teacher defined (i.e. they are entering *your* space, with *your* expectations), then pulling them back will inevitably be a challenge. Have them line up and settle outside, before they enter and sit down. Or at the very least, make a point of greeting them as they come through the door, in a welcoming but strong, business-like manner – setting the tone for the rest of the lesson. For more ideas see Chapter 4 on Organising the classroom.

Key points for whole-class low-level disruption:
> Awareness of behaviour triggers will help you to tackle problems in a meaningful way.
> Recognise that some triggers can be controlled by you, but others can't – don't blame yourself if you feel like you are fighting a loosing battle.
> Do, however, be honest with yourself when reflecting on your approach towards your pupils.
> If you are faced with very challenging pupils, don't be afraid to ask for help and support.
> Keep your interventions firm but low level. Overreacting early on will give you fewer options if behaviour deteriorates, and can lead to resentment and/or ridicule.
> Focus on reacting through skill rather than emotion.
> Be persistent and consistent in your approach – change may not happen overnight, but once pupils realise that you are not giving up, they will.
> Explore preventative ways of reducing low-level disruption, such as using starter activities, routines and reward systems.

Self-esteem

The words 'low self-esteem' form an oft-repeated tag line for pupils displaying challenging behaviours and disaffection. It's not that I don't agree with this, but I think it is not enough to simply say 'oh . . . he's got very low self-esteem, that explains his antics'. The true challenge is in understanding what it is to have low self-esteem and how it affects an individual's relationship with the world. It is a complex issue, yet one that lies at the heart of many classroom problems.

Self-esteem can be regarded as the sum of a set of judgements about one's value, worthiness and competence. It can also be defined as having two distinct elements: *self-belief* and *self-worth*.

- *Self-belief* concerns the idea that an individual has skills, talents and competencies to offer to the world.
- *Self-worth* relates to a sense of personal validity, that the individual feels loved and wanted in the world.

It is possible to have unbalanced levels of either. Typical examples include the over-achiever (high self-belief, low self-worth); who, despite constantly proving themselves, perhaps in sport, academically, or even socially, never truly feels they have done enough – because of a deep underlying sense that they are unworthy or 'unlovable'. Such individuals can be prone to depression and issues such as eating disorders. This is what a member of the discussion group had to say:

> I was the sort of pupil who would always get my homework in on time, and would always be striving for top marks. On one level this was good because I did very well at school, but I also put a lot of pressure on myself, and if I felt like I wasn't living up to expectations, which happened often, I would be very self-critical and unhappy. I don't know if my teachers were aware of this or not; as far as they were concerned I was simply their star student.

In contrast, you may have encountered a number of pupils who exhibit arrogant, cock-sure behaviour, and could easily assume that they are simply 'full of themselves'. In reality such attitude can be typical of an individual who has high self-worth (feels important in the world), but low self-belief (insecurities about their skills). All that showing-off and intimidation is bravado: an armour designed to conceal deep-rooted fears of failure.

Reflection box:
Consider one or several pupils in your class. Based on how you have seen them behave and relate to others, can you see traits of low self-worth/belief in them? Does this make you feel differently towards the challenges they present to you?

Although every individual has her/his own set of personal circumstances that will affect her/his self-esteem, areas for consideration may include the following:

Socio/economic status
Media pressure
Belonging to a minority ethnic community
Gender
Academic achievement
Bullying
Appearance
Parents

The final one on the list will, no doubt, see a few nodding heads. Research suggests that parents are indeed a key influence on the self-esteem of their offspring. As well as the genetic factor, parenting style plays a significant role. The most damaging thing a parent can do is abuse (physically, sexually or emotionally), but family conflict, instability and breakdown is also an issue.

Of course, as a teacher, your role is not to provide social work or family therapy, it is to teach; but you can gain strength from at least having an awareness of the challenges that young people are contending with. This awareness allows you to empathise and to put undesirable behaviour into context, in other words, to not take it personally.

What sort of challenging behaviours would we typically associate with low self-esteem? Arguably most of them, but the teachers and school staff I have worked with, raised the following as common examples:

General disengagement with school life
Fear of failure/task anxiety
Work avoidance tactics (i.e. mucking around) as a way of coping
    with the above

Depression
Alcohol, drug or substance abuse
Eating disorders
Self-harm
Stealing
Bullying
Social isolation or reluctance to join in
Loss of concentration, and/or loss of interest in activities
Refusal to go to school, or take part in certain activities
Extreme irritability and moodiness
Self-criticism
Attention-seeking behaviour
Excessively confident, pushy or arrogant behaviour (compensating for low self-belief)
Undue aggression

The signs of low self-esteem can be evident even in very young children and toddlers, as well as primary school children and teenagers.

The next concern is then to be: what can 'perfect' teachers do about low self-esteem in their classrooms? Although it may feel like an issue that is largely beyond our control, we do have scope to make a difference. This point was brought to me, by an unexpected visit from an ex-pupil at the behaviour unit where I used to work. I remembered the boy, now a young adult, as soon as he appeared on the doorstep – how could I forget? He gave us absolute hell for three years, whilst we did our best to reinforce positive messages about right and wrong and taking responsibility for your self. His response when I greeted him was incredibly warm: 'You people were good to me. You were the only ones that ever helped me.' Hmm . . . it didn't feel like that at the time.

Part of the intriguing – and frustrating – thing about being a teacher is that you may never find out what effect you have had on your pupils and it may well be more significant than you think.

Reflection box:
What can you remember about your own teachers when you were at school? Are there any incidents or conversations that particularly stand out? What effect do you think they have had on you?

Simple measures you can take in your classroom to encourage positive self-esteem amongst your pupils include the following:

- Giving frequent praise, but making it meaningful (see section on Rewards and sanctions).
- Noticing improvements as well as achievements.
- Using a personalised reward system that recognises individual successes.
- Never making unkind personal remarks or criticisms – even in a joking way, and even if students do it to you.
- Avoiding singling out shy or withdrawn students or putting them 'on the spot' in front of the whole-class.
- Promoting an ethos in which everyone is valued: explain that people have different strengths and weaknesses, different skills and different rates of working.
- Encouraging pupils to explore their strengths through joining clubs that they will enjoy and that will raise their confidence, for example sports, drama, music, art, computers.
- Creating opportunities for pupils to engage with each other in a positive way, for example circle time, drama and role-play activities, team-building activities.
- Giving pupils focused, personal attention, which can be as simple as greeting them in the corridor, or having a casual conversation about their interests.
- Keeping aware of more serious problems, such as drug abuse eating disorders, self-harm and depression, and taking appropriate action, for example alerting parents, head of year, school counsellor, etc.

Key points for self-esteem:
- > Be sensitive to the impact that low self-esteem can have on a young person's attitudes and behaviours.
- > Remember that even the loud-mouthed show offs may well be using this to conceal deep-rooted insecurities.
- > Think of aggressive behaviour as the outward expression of inner anger and upset – some people are able to talk about their problems, others find this extremely hard.
- > Simple things can help to make your class a positive, welcoming space: smiling, giving praise, showing an interest in your pupils.

Rewards and sanctions

Structure plays a valuable role in any classroom, and is particularly important when it comes to behaviour management. Both you and your pupils will feel more calm and secure if each of you has a clear sense of what is and isn't acceptable within the classroom, and an understanding of how problems will be dealt with. If boundaries are frequently and consistently reinforced, the chances of something getting out of hand, or going 'too far' are reduced. Structure is reassuring, and one simple way to provide it is by having a clear system of rewards and sanctions (or consequences).

To me, good behaviour management has to be about encouraging pupils to manage their own behaviour, and to take responsibility for their actions. To support this, I try to offer my pupils choice, for example: 'You need to concentrate on your work or you will have to move to the front desk. It's your choice.' This approach encourages pupils to identify with the cause and effect of their behaviours (which otherwise seems to allude many of them!). It also creates breathing space for those individuals who are stubborn or who dislike being backed into a corner, therefore reducing the risk of a power-seeking conflict. But above all, it gives pupils the option to turn their situation around, to indeed 'make the right choice', and hopefully to realise that it's down to them: ultimately *they* have control over the way their life turns out.

> **Reflection box:**
> How often do you find yourself getting drawn into an argument with a pupil because she/he is refusing to do something you've told her/him to do? What do you think the argument is motivated by? Who wins?

The use of choice can be reinforced with rewards and sanctions, depending, of course, on which pathway the pupil takes: option one leads to wonderful joy and happiness, option two leads to certain doom! Judging by the feedback from teachers and staff, most schools and/or classrooms have some kind of reward and sanction system in place. These range from whole-school merit schemes, to individual teachers offering jelly babies to the worthy. But how successful are they? And what effect do they have on pupils' intrinsic motivation to do the right thing?

One thing everyone agreed on is that the effectiveness of rewards and sanctions depends on getting 'em where it matters. A reward is only a reward if it is something you want or that you will benefit from; likewise a sanction is only going to bother you if it causes you some level of inconvenience. An ex-primary school pupil described how:

> In the summer term, every year group worked towards going on a day trip. Unfortunately the suitable places near us were fairly limited, and so we had to rely on the same things again and again. In our final year loads of us started to misbehave so that we could get out of it – we just couldn't face another visit to the local wildlife park.

Tastes and interests change over time and with age. If you use a system that offers tangible incentives such as trips or prizes, these incentives need to have appeal. They also need to have a level of simplicity about them; that makes them realistic and convenient for you to deliver. I know a lot of teenagers who appreciate phone credit and music vouchers – money talks – but who's going to pay for it? Unless your school invests financially in rewarding pupils, or has some means of funding it, don't spend your own money – the costs quickly build up. Other issues to consider regarding reward systems include the following:

> *Whole school or personal to your classroom?* Whole-school systems of awarding points/merits/stars/certificates/etc. can be effective, but only if all staff consistently make use of them, which is quite a feat in a large school. Such systems can easily become devalued if pupils do not think it's 'cool' to receive a merit, which often happens higher up the school. The benefit of a classroom reward systems is that it can be tailored to your style and your pupils, and is much easier for you to keep track of; however, it may lack the grand impact of a whole-school system, and you will need to make sure that it doesn't clash or compromise other teacher approaches.
>
> *Tangible prize or intrinsic reward?* This is a tricky one. Part of me likes to think that the most important rewards are the simplest (such as personal attention, praise or a pleasant thank you), but unfortunately these are often the ones that are taken for

granted. Also, I have had such great results when using external motivators, such as working towards a class trip – I know they can work. Perhaps the answer is to provide both: plenty of meaningful praise and attention throughout the year, with a prize provided for special situations or occasions (even 'perfect' teachers need gimmicks sometimes!).

What sort of rewards work best? Ones that are free to you (or cost you *very* little), and are easy and quick to provide. Stickers or stamps can be effective, even with older pupils. Notes, certificates or post cards home can also work well, as can the occasional phone-call. Some staff suggested handing out grapes or sweets or small items of stationery, which is fine, as long as your school policy accepts it. I have also found giving pupils some relaxation time at the end of a lesson, or the chance to play some music, is very effective – when a reward is close in time to the incident that earned it, it has greater impact. With regards to tangible prizes, bear in mind that if everyone is competing towards one grand prize (I have known of mountain bikes to be on offer), this will automatically put off the pupils it should be trying to reach (the ones that know they'll never be top of the class) – better to have lots of little prizes, or one that includes everyone, such as a trip or activity.

Individual or group rewards? A competitive element can really motivate pupils (for instance, working in teams to earn the most points throughout a lesson). It does, however, run the risk of isolating unpopular or difficult individuals, and will put off the easily defeated (see above). Rewards that acknowledge individual efforts, achievements and improvements are a safer option, allowing you the flexibility to encourage everyone for different reasons. For example, a points chart with each pupil's name: once pupils get to a certain number of points, they receive a prize or certificate. The criteria for earning points can remain flexible and/or can be aimed at specific things (e.g. handing in homework, completing work, etc.). A simple, broad system like this can cover everything, and avoids the over-complication of having different rewards for different situations, such as lining-up points, work points, help points, etc.

As with rewards, the most effective sanctions are those that are simple and as close to the incident as possible, so that pupils can clearly recognise that the choices they made over their behaviour lead directly to the consequences. Again, you may be expected to work within your school's system of sanctioning pupils; which is great if it's an effective one, frustrating if it's not. So what makes for an effective system of sanctions? Naturally, this depends on the nature of the school and its pupils, but within my research, several key themes emerged:

- *System has a sliding scale*: after a difficulty, the pupil gets referred up the school, for example teacher fills in a simple slip, which is passed on and the problem is then taken up by another, possibly senior, member of staff. If the behaviour is serious or recurring, information can be passed up the scale, leading to head teacher intervention or interview with parents.
- *Uniformity*: if such a system is adopted and maintained through-out the school, at every level, it establishes a consistency of expectation, and demonstrates to pupils that staff are unified and that things *do* get dealt with. It also provides recorded evidence of behavioural issues, which can be useful for pre-senting to parents (and exclusion panels).
- *Teacher stays in the loop*: everyone agreed that, in a system where issues are passed on, the teacher who initially deals with the incident should be involved, as much as possible, with developments and outcomes; thereby suggesting to the pupil that she/he is just as influential and important within the school, as senior staff are. The same goes for the next point.
- *Apologies/reconciliation before re-entry*: it is a point that I insist upon, for the benefit of both the teacher and the pupil. The pupil needs to be reminded that she/he is accountable for her/his actions, and this involves facing up to the people that she/he has affected or upset. The teacher needs to feel empowered and satisfied that the pupil has taken this on board.

On this issue one teacher explained:

I know we are always supposed to be forgiving, but it drives me mad when I see teachers not having their viewpoint or dignity respected, for the sake of getting the pupil back into class. I was once called some very offensive names by a male pupil. He was sent out, but twenty minutes later the teacher in charge brought him back, and after saying sorry on his behalf, she pressured me to have him in the room again. The boy knew he'd got away with it, and sat there smirking at me for the rest of the lesson. I was furious.

Besides a whole-school system of sanction, other types of sanction that teachers and school staff said they made use of were as follows:

Detentions
Punishment exercise (e.g. lines, copying out text)
Litter duty
Tidying up the classroom
Threatening to, or actually, phoning parents
Withdrawal of privileges (e.g. sitting with friends, taking part in activities or trips)
Removing pupil's shoe (dubious at best)
Writing names on board

Caution was raised by several people; suggesting that sanctions cannot provide the ultimate solution to behavioural problems. There will always be a collection of individuals who seem indifferent to whatever sanctions they are given, and one has to wonder why it is often the same pupils that land up in detention time and time again – somewhere along the line the method isn't working. An experienced teaching assistant suggested that the most 'perfect' teachers they worked with would use detentions very sparingly:

Five minutes during break or lunch, or at the end of the day, which involved a short, sharp discussion about the pupils' behaviour. Because the teachers already had the pupils' respect, that was enough to make a difference.

Long, formal detentions can easily become a time-drain on staff, which is especially frustrating if they are failing to have an impact (i.e. pupils who are always in detention, or who repeatedly fail to turn up). That said, if the school behaviour policy promotes the use of detentions and/or has found them to be effective, the 'perfect' teacher should endeavour to uphold this – which brings us back to the point about uniformity. For behaviour management to have an impact, especially in tougher schools, staff have to stick together. They have to back each other up, and demonstrate to pupils that they are working in conjunction with each other. Otherwise, the whole system is weakened. A head teacher warned:

> It frustrates me when certain teachers start complaining about the behaviour of the pupils. Inevitably they come to me and say 'what are you going to do about it?' and I think 'well, I've done something already – go and look at our behaviour policy!' Importantly, my staff are all made aware of this policy; most of them make use of it, and are happy. It's always the same few who don't bother with it, or think they would be better off doing their own thing – and they are the ones who think there are problems.

Perhaps the secret of the perfect teacher is that she/he shares and promotes the common values of the school, whilst still displaying her/his own individual flair for the role – balancing the personal instinct to build relationships with pupils with the civic duty to stick to the procedures. Personally, I believe that behaviour management strategies, including rewards and sanctions, are absolutely worthless, unless the teacher in question endeavours to build some kind of rapport with the students in the first place (see Chapter 5, section on Relationships with teaching colleagues). If this rapport is strong and based on respect, the need for strategies is likely to be reduced anyway.

Rewards and sanctions play a role in supporting effective behaviour management, but they are not a substitute for positive, constructive pupil/teacher relationships.

Key points for rewards and sanctions:
> ➤ A clear system of rewards and consequences can help provide structure to your classroom management approach.

> Keep them simple and realistic – don't promise/threaten what you cannot deliver.
> If you are using tangible rewards they need to be motivating (e.g. music/cinema vouchers) but simple things like stickers and stamps can also have an effect.
> Be aware that motivations can change over time – what works with some pupils may not work with others.
> Rewards and consequence have most effect when they are swift and are close to the achievement/difficulty itself – so that the connection is clear.
> The most meaningful reward is arguably giving a pupil your positive attention and praise.
> Consistency matters – work with other staff to agree on key classroom behaviour boundaries, so that you can back each other up and send a clear message to pupils.
> Remember that rewards and consequences are not a replacement for good general behaviour management and de-escalation skills.

Establishing boundaries

Effective behaviour management starts with boundaries: deciding and defining where the line between what is and is not acceptable lies. We've all heard pious parents and teachers remarking along the lines of: 'Oh, so-and-so would be fine if he only had some *boundaries* . . .' The consensus seems to be that boundaries are something that children and young people need and benefit from, regardless of whether they act indifferently towards them. Arguably, a significant proportion of challenging behaviour is the result of pupils trying to test and finding out where those boundaries are, to re-enforce that sense of control and enclosure – a sense that is perhaps synonymous with feelings of safety and security. A behaviour support worker explains:

My pupils have a particular knack of testing new people to their limits. If anyone comes to the school, they will ask impertinent questions and give constant challenge, and if they get away with it, which they often do, because they seem so intimidating, they will push further – it becomes a spiral of destruction and

time-wasting which they feel they are controlling. If the boundaries come down early on, and they are directed away from that
spiral, they tend to remain calmer and happier. They definitely
show more respect towards people who know not to let them
get away with it.

Reflection box:

When do you draw the line? How far do you allow pupils to
go before you pull them up on their behaviour? What are the
factors that affect this (e.g. anxieties about pupil reaction, not
enough time to deal with problem, too busy with other issues)?

Boundaries are present in all areas of society (although some
might suggest not enough) to manage and control our behaviour.
Within the classroom, boundaries should exist to serve the pupils
and the staff, making the environment a safe, productive and positive one. Some of these are to be artificially imposed (such as class
rules and codes of behaviour), but many are expected to be intrinsic within our natures – a moral understanding of what is right and
wrong; or of wanting to help, rather than hinder, progress.

However, judging by comments from my discussion group, it is
perhaps a fallacy to assume that, in the twenty-first-century classroom, intrinsic codes of behaviour, such as morality, manners and
consideration of others, are automatically in place for our pupils.
Whether this is because behaviour standards at large are slipping
(which is hence reflected in schools), or because 'social' education
has been squeezed out of the timetable by an attainment-driven
curriculum, or because children are simply being children, inexperienced and raw and requiring guidance through life, is a matter of
on-going debate. But we cannot, as one teacher explains, take for
granted that pupils will arrive at school with an implicit sense of
positive, fair and socially acceptable behaviour:

> When I first started teaching at nursery level, I was shocked by
> how much time I had to spend helping pupils learn about shar-
> ing and being kind to one another . . . when I became a Year 6
> teacher, I was even more shocked to discover that I still had to
> spend lots of time on these things. They were worse than the
> little ones!

So what can the 'perfect' teacher do to establish and re-enforce boundaries within her/his classroom? The logical place to start is in the setting up of an agreed selection of rules/rights, or a classroom code of behaviour. This helps to make your expectations explicit and can be referred to as necessary, reminding pupils of their rules/rights whenever issues arise. Perhaps one of the key benefits of having a code of behaviour is that it protects the relationship between staff and pupils: it separates you from the problems. In other words, in matters of discipline, it is not you nagging at your pupils; it is simply what is stated in the rules. And if these rules have been agreed by consensus, this has even more impact. A learning mentor explains:

> We agree on the rules at the start of the year, and everyone signs a contract. Pupils tend to be enthusiastic and have lots of suggestions, so it is not hard to get them on board. It works very well when someone mucks about or complains that something is unfair, and staff are able to say, 'well, these are the rules that *you* wanted!'

If there is one thing that young people seem to care about, it is 'fairness'. It was a recurring sticking point within my discussion group, with a feeling that teachers who were inconsistent in their approach, or who imposed their decisions without justifying them (i.e. 'do as I tell you to, or else') were unreasonable and 'out of order'. Therefore, open discussion about rules/rights and behaviour expectations with your class will help to give them a sense of ownership and responsibility, and help them to feel that their opinions are valued. A primary school pupil commented:

> I hate it when my teacher lets some kids do things, and tells others off. She is moody and gets really angry with us for no reason. (Does she have class rules?). She has them, but no one cares . . . because she tells us off whenever she likes anyway.

Sounds like a case of a teacher that has come to the end of her tether – and is now reacting through her (frazzled) emotions rather than through her professional skill. It can happen to us all, but the consequences are inevitable: pupils will lose faith and respect for someone whom they feel they cannot trust and make sense of.

Here are some suggestions on how to make your code of behaviour effective and easy to maintain:

- *Keep it in the classroom consciousness*: ensure that expectations are regularly circulated by referring to them frequently ('Remember our rule about . . .') and making a visual display of them. This suggests to pupils that the code matters.
- *Use it consistently (but use your judgement)*: pupils want fairness, and will be quickly disillusioned if they think some individuals get away with more than others do. However, experiences teaches us that it is necessary to maintain a bit of flexibility, for example, in understanding the context of an incident and knowing the nature and issues of the individuals involved.
- *Make rules/rights simple*: keep them straightforward, positive and purposeful and have as few as possible. For example:

In this classroom we (the pupils and the staff) have the right:

1. To respect
2. To learn and to teach
3. To feel safe

These can be applied to a broad range of problems, and the dual ownership (they relate to both pupils and staff) avoids creating an atmosphere of 'us and them'.

- *Make rules easy to follow*: if pupils are given ultimatums it could possibly lead to confrontation or refusal to cooperate (see section on Key points for resolving conflicts). Presenting a choice ('You need to follow our rule about . . . or you will have to . . .'), and using a system of warnings will encourage complicity.

So what should these rules be? This is a matter of individual concern, and should also relate to the needs and issues of your particular classroom environment. For example, if you teach a practical subject, you will have to take account of the health and safety issues. If you have very challenging classes, you may find that a simple but broad set of rules (that cover many different behaviour problems) will be more effective and easier to manage than lots of little specific ones. You may want to have rules for specific situations, such as lining up, break-times or getting out equipment.

It is also important to consider your class rules in the context of whole-school rules – do they support each other? Whole-school unity is the bedrock of successful whole-school behaviour management, but it can be difficult to maintain if everyone has an individual approach. We are not robots; we cannot suck the personality and individuality out of ourselves entirely just for the sake consistency – the pupils would miss out on some wonderful teachers! Yet there needs to be some common ground, agreed basics. The best way to start achieving this is to get everyone involved in the decision-making process, and to have the school behaviour policy openly and regularly reviewed to ensure that people are happy and confident about its principles.

Reflection box:
What matters to you? Your code of behaviour will be easier to reinforce if it represents your values, but do your values fit in with the rest of the schools? For example, how do you feel about issues such as swearing? How does your school deal with swearing?

Key points for establishing boundaries:
> Young people need and benefit from boundaries. Don't be put off if/when they try to fight against them.
> Encourage complicity and responsibility by involving pupils in the process of decided what the rules/rights of the classroom are.
> Some individuals will need more support in valuing and following boundaries than others – law-abiding behaviour cannot be taken for granted.
> Keep rules simple, positive and limited in number – making them easier to follow. General rules (e.g. 'we have the right to respect') can cover lots of issues, but specific rules (e.g. 'we

must walk slowly in the corridors'), can be useful for specific situations.

> When establishing classroom rules, consider how they reflect and support whole-school rules.

Resolving conflicts

Confrontation with pupils is perhaps something that every teacher dreads – understandably, for it can be stressful and frustrating. It can also form a potential threat to our status, and status is not something to be taken lightly. Indeed, from observations and discussions, it seems to me, that the teachers most likely to get entangled in arguments are those that are concerned about the image they portray to their pupils, or more precisely, the appearance of 'power'. A head of year explained:

> I have to admit . . . I have given myself problems in the past . . . I have never been physically aggressive, but I know how to intimidate pupils in order to get them to follow my way – the classic army major. Sometimes it seems like the easiest option . . . but every now and then, I've had pupils who try it on. My immediate reaction is 'how dare they!' and that's where it starts to break down . . . if they push my limits I automatically want to push theirs . . . I have to work hard to control my own temper.

If only all teachers were this honest and self-aware. Power, or rather the pursuit of it, is a risky thing in the classroom. We have all come across those volatile little darlings who like to argue that day is night, or who seem to have an innate aversion to doing what they have been asked to do. But however frustrating their inclinations may be, trying to 'control' through domination or force can easily lead to conflict – they want to remain in power as much as we do. And who wins the struggle? The one who doesn't have to keep their professional dignity intact.

So how can the perfect teacher successfully manage her/his pupils, including the difficult ones, without having to resort to arguments and power games? Perhaps the best way to resolve a conflict is to prevent it from starting in the first place. Awareness of what is happening in the classroom, and of individual needs and temperaments, is the place to start.

Reflection box:
How do you know when/where problems are developing? What are the early-warning signs that pupils are getting wound up? Agitated chatter and raised voices? Increased fidgeting? Moving around the room? Going quiet?

If you know your pupils and know what to watch out for, you will be able to intervene early or even anticipate potential problems, and therefore deal with them before they escalate out of control. From there, it is a matter of developing the skills to be able to diffuse these tense situations. There are a number of things you can do:

- *Remain calm yourself:* if you approach pupils with a calm and confident manner you are much more likely to de-escalate and stabilise difficult situations (see section on Creating calm). Keep you voice low and quiet, but firm, and resist any personal comments. Think professionally, express empathy: 'I can see that there's a problem here . . .' If you have the knack, humour can be an excellent way if diffusing things. Smaller children (and sometimes older ones!) can also respond well to distraction: engaging them in an activity or conversation that is nothing to do with their problem, diverts their attention, and thereby calms them down.
- *Think about your body language:* what does a calm person look like? Relaxed. Small, open hand gestures. Being discreet. Firm but friendly. Getting down to the pupils eye level, but at the same time, observing their need for personal space – not blocking their way or closing in on them.
- *Don't react or get entangled:* sometimes pupils may deliberately try to draw you into an argument or make personal comments designed to upset and disarm you. Whilst it may be appropriate to challenge such behaviour after the event, your initial reaction should imply that you will not rise to such

provoking, so try to be business like and use neutral come-
backs such as 'Those sort of comments aren't of interest to
me' or 'That's fine, we can talk about that later, but for now
I need to see you calming down.' If necessary move away,
and focus your attention on the pupils that are doing the
right things.

- *Avoid giving ultimatums*: people are more likely to become
  confrontational if they feel they are being backed into a
  corner, or being controlled (the 'power struggle'). We cannot *force* our pupils to do anything, but we can increase our
  chances of gaining their cooperation if we allow them to
  maintain some control over their actions by giving one or
  two warnings (providing a 'way out') and offering choice,
  for example 'You need to step outside the room and calm
  down for a few minutes, or I'm afraid you will have to go to
  the office'.

- *Keep things simple and on point*: communication becomes
  harder when we are under stress; so talk clearly, make expectations as obvious and explicit as possible, avoid ambiguous
  or unnecessary phrases, and avoid bringing up past issues and
  problems. Focus on the immediate issues.

- *Try to focus on positives*: support pupils to move away from
  confrontation by giving reassurance and guidance on how
  they can put things right. This is easier if you know the pupil
  and know what the root cause of the difficulty may be, for
  example, anxiety about not being able to do a particular task
  or conflict with another pupil.

- *Allow for 'take-up' time*: pupils, particularly those with a defiant
  streak, will be more likely to comply with teacher instructions if the pressure, and the audience, is taken away. Give a
  pupil her/his warning/instruction, and then take your attention elsewhere (i.e. to the rest of the class) for a few minutes,
  before revisiting.

This last point is simple but very valuable. From my experiences
observing teachers, it seems that one of the common agitators of
classroom conflict is a mood of impatience. Understandably, many
teachers may feel that they have limited time to get through
the work and to deal with all that they have to deal with; and

therefore, will feel under pressure to get pupils to comply with their instructions right there and then. There is no time for arguing or waiting. Rather than allowing the pupil some time and space to come round, they may be urged to hover over them and say what needs to be said several times in several different ways. A secondary teacher explains:

> My worst habit use to be nagging pupils . . . I would really get on their case, thinking that if I put enough pressure on, they would give in quickly. If they argued back . . . I'd have them sent out. Over the years, I discovered that if I made my request once, firmly, and then left them alone, the chances are, I would turn around to find out that they'd done it – saving a lot of time and argument along the way.

Not all classroom conflict involves clashes with teachers. In fact, some of the most daunting situations occur when pupils are clashing with each other: arguments, insults, threats and fights. And anyone who has ever had to deal with such a situation will know how quickly the drama can escalate. What starts as seemingly friendly banter can quickly bubble over, and suddenly pupils are on their feet, shouting and squaring up to one another across the classroom. What do you do?

As has been aforementioned, the key to managing rising conflict is to diffuse it at the earliest possible stage; intervening *before* things get out of control. It is helpful to know or to anticipate potential triggers (i.e. pupils who don't get on, issues around school, historical grudges) so that you are at least a little bit prepared; therefore communicate and share information with other staff. A teaching assistant explains the system that works in her school:

> We have an information sheet on one of the staff-room notice boards which highlights things to look out for around school . . . pupils falling out, bullying issues, tensions between different groups – it really helps staff to be vigilant, and the amount of incidents has definitely decreased.

When sparks start to fly, react swiftly, and focus on getting some distance between the individuals involved, so that the argument/

trade of insults cannot continue. Once the cycle of confrontation is broken (i.e. pupils are separated from one another), it will be much easier to establish the origins of the problem, to calm the individuals down and move towards a resolution. Here is where staff teamwork comes into play – separating potential brawlers is more straightforward if you have places to send them for a cooling off period (e.g. another classroom or staffed area of the school). Otherwise, you may have to send one outside and keep one with you in class, which at least gives you some room to deal with pupils separately, before attempting to bring them back together.

Occasionally fights may happen so quickly and so suddenly that early intervention is not an option. Most fights, although distressing, will actually fizzle out, often of their own accord, or through the actions of noble classmates. Nonetheless, a number of school staff in my discussion group had, at some point, felt the need to physically intervene.

Reflection box:
If a fight broke out in front of you, how would you deal with it? Would you feel confident that you could successfully break it up? What are the factors that would determine your decision to do this?

With increasing concern about violence in society and for pupils carrying weapons such us knives into schools, the question of physically intervening is one that may need careful consideration. But beyond the media hype, it is also a matter of understanding the full implications of your decision before you wade in:

- *What does your school policy say*? Every school should provide guidelines for physical intervention as part of their behaviour policy. If you have not seen it or been made aware of it, ask.
- *Have you had suitable training*? Physical intervention training will give you confidence, and also the assurance that you have a framework of legal backup (because accusations can happen), providing your actions are within the course guidelines and demonstrate use of judgement. A good course will focus on de-escalation skills (physical intervention is a last

resort), guidance on legislation and codes of practice, and risk assessments, as well as teaching sound, safe techniques.

Physical intervention is, of course, a reactive measure. I am always in favour, as I'm sure all the other aspiring 'perfect' teachers out there are, of practice that *prevents* problems from happening in the first place. The general culture and atmosphere of a school can have a significant impact on the amount of aggression that takes place within its walls. A parent explains:

> We moved my son out of his previous school because he was constantly coming home with stories about fights and violence between pupils . . . His new school is only down the road from the old one, but it's a different world. It has a strong ethos of respect, and it feels like a friendly, pleasant place to be. I have no doubt that teachers work really hard to maintain this, but the benefits are obvious.

If a school values respectful behaviour, and places it at the fore-front of its culture as well as promoting positive ways of solving difficulties, confrontation and aggression will inevitably decrease. This, in turn, will allow more time for teaching and learning and the raising of aspirations. And in some ways, it is also relatively simple: just be nice to each other. The 'perfect' teacher, of course, does this effortlessly. For the rest of us, we can start by modelling friendly manners and praising the like. When necessary, we can help pupils solve their disputes, by taking the time to talk through their issues with them and developing their awareness of the alternatives to fighting and squabbling. Also, in the way we manage our day-to-day teaching activities, we can encourage social skills such as turn taking, sharing, helping one other, giving praise and compliments, being assertive, and communicating.

Reflection box:

What do you do to promote respectful, considerate behaviour in your classroom? How do you support pupils in solving their arguments and difficulties? Do you encourage them to look after one another? Do you praise kind, helpful behaviour?

Key points for resolving conflict:

> - Keep a check on your own manner in the classroom – are you a confrontational person that finds it difficult to walk away from an argument?
> - Don't take personal comments personally – it's not worth it, and if some pupils think they've discovered a chink in your armour they may try to use it against you.
> - Keep an eye out for signs of rising tensions, and intervene early on, using a calm, low-level approach (e.g. quietly asking if there's a problem).
> - Avoid getting drawn into arguments by being business like and moving away.
> - Give pupils 'take-up time', allowing them to follow your expectations away from the pressure.
> - It is good practice to share relevant information with other staff and raise awareness of any conflicts between pupils.
> - Get to grips with your school's behaviour policy, and ensure that you know how and who to contact should you need help in an emergency.
> - Promote friendship and respect towards others in your class-room, and model good examples.

4 Organising the classroom

Creating a learning space

I have always believed that the appearance and organisation of the physical environment that you teach in can make a valuable difference to the atmosphere of your lessons. Teaching in a space that is messy and cluttered can create distractions, as well as wasted time, having to hunt around for resources and equipment. A space that is tatty and uncared for gives the message that the learning space isn't valued, which will do little to boost the motivation of the pupils (and the staff). A space that is drab and impersonal may feel unwelcoming, making it hard for yourself and your pupils to feel proud and responsible for it.

Alternatively, think of the classroom that is orderly and tidy: where things have their place, and pupils are encouraged to put them back when they've finished using them. Imagine the displays, which are bold and interesting, and reflect the learning going on in the classroom. The 'perfect' teacher's classroom has personality, but also order: you should be able to look across the space and see the pupils and their desks, rather than have your vision distracted by one-day-it-might-be-useful bric-a-brac, piles of scrap paper and last year's teaching files left lying on the sideboards.

A London head teacher had this to say about the experience of visiting different classrooms within her school:

> It concerns me to see classrooms that are in a mess. I understand that they are busy places, and cannot be always be pristine, but if the untidiness is ongoing I have to ask myself why. It makes

me wonder whether the teacher responsible for that room is on top of things in general.

Reflection box:

What state is your classroom in? Could it benefit from a clear out? Does it need refreshing? Ask you pupils what they feel about it and what improvements they would like to see.

Chaotic classroom space creates stress, and makes that all-important challenge of managing low-level disruption more difficult. Spotting the pupil that is out of place or off task will be trickier if there is a sea of clutter getting in the way. Also, if there are things lying about on desks and sideboards, there is increased temptation lying in the pathway of pupils who tend to fidget, tap, flick or fiddle with things. If you feel your room is in need of tidying-up, get pupils involved in the process – if they are playing an active part in the maintenance of classroom order, they will feel more pride and respect for it in the long term. Here are some suggestions:

- If you are new to a classroom, spend a few weeks working in it, as it is – get to know the space, before you make key decisions about what to change and where to store things.
- Be ruthless when clearing out. Organise items into three categories: 'keep', 'maybe' and 'chuck'. Go through the 'maybe' pile a second time, and be firm with yourself.
- One person's waste is another person's treasure. Write up a list of items you no longer want and place it on the staff-room notice board – you might be surprised to discover what other people can make use of!
- Arrange for poster and signs to be laminated, which will preserve their lifespan, and have a neater appearance.
- Organise stationery and small resources into clearly labelled trays, and have helpers/classroom monitors take responsibility for maintaining their good order.
- Get into the habit of incorporating tidying-up time into your lesson structure, ensuring that it is done routinely.
- Promote clear expectations about having respect for the environment and for resources.

- Make your classroom 'greener': set up a recycling station for scrap paper and other items.
- Keep the focal point of the classroom (from where you do most of your teaching) as plain and clutter-free as possible, minimising distractions.

Of course, you may not have the luxury of your own classroom space, or perhaps the one you have has to be shared with several others. This is commonplace in secondary schools, and requires, at times, a bit of diplomacy and good organisational skills. Your subject may also require that you teach in a certain kind of space, for example, a laboratory or workshop; and that you manage specific resources, such as tools or computer equipment. These factors bring their own set of concerns. A science teacher explains:

In my subject I have to place heavy emphasis on ground-rules, in order to make sure that equipment is being used safely and sensibly. With younger pupils it sometimes feels like they need constant reminders. Older pupils tend to be more respectful, because over the years they have learned that looking after things means they can be trusted to do more interesting activities.

Around school, there are all kinds of people who can help you to manage your resources and get the best out of equipment, for example, technicians, subject coordinators and site managers. If you regularly rely on technology to deliver your lessons, such as an interactive whiteboard, and if, like me, you tend to have a jinx effect on hard drives, it truly pays to have good relations with your ICT technician!

Reflection box:
Are your resources working hard enough for you? Do you know exactly what is available to you and where it is kept? Are you making the most of any allocated budget?

In the 'perfect' teacher's classroom, function and orderliness also needed to be supported by efforts to make the classroom a bright, pleasant and inspirational space to be in. A secondary school pupil highlights this:

> I hate being in some of the classrooms . . . because they are cold and really dull, and they're painted in horrible colours, like beige. I like being in lessons where teachers have made the room look nice . . . so that if you're bored, you can look at the stuff on the walls.

Hmmm.

As has been aforementioned, a room needs to have a bit of 'personality'. The obvious way to do this is, is through thoughtful displays. These can be used to promote themes and topics that are being studied, to show off pupils' work, to reinforce classroom rules and expectations, or for sharing information. If you teach one class (e.g. in a primary or special school), or your classroom is used as a registration group form room, consider allocating some of the display area for sharing information, photographs, birthdays, etc. If pupils feel they have some ownership over the space, they will hopefully have more pride in it.

Key points for creating a learning space:
> - A tidy, organised space reflects well on your general teaching abilities and is an easier environment to control – less stress.
> - Involving pupils in maintaining classroom tidiness encourages them to see the value of resources and to treat things with respect.
> - Display work or photographs that will encourage pupils to feel a sense of ownership over the space, and create a more welcoming atmosphere.
> - Before you set about sticking things up on the walls or ceiling, check your school's policy, and be clear about what you can and cannot do – some schools are adverse to materials such us blue-tack or sticky tape, due to the damage they cause to paintwork and plaster.
> - And you don't want to annoy the site manager because . . . get to know the useful people within the school, for example site managers and technicians, who may be able to do you the odd favour.

> Be aware of the health and safety issues that relate to your subject and the equipment you use.

Setting up routines

Routines are an inevitable part of school life. Pupils need them, to feel secure and reassured of their boundaries. Staff need them, in order to feel confident in what they are doing, and to know that they are supported by some sort of structure. Get routines right, keep them simple, and they should make things easier. If, however, they are over-complicated or unclear, they can become unwieldy and counterproductive. I am always in favour of simplicity. I make this point, because I realise that sometimes it is difficult to stick even to the basics – if there are a lot of things going on around you at once, you don't need the added pressure of trying to make sure pupils are following a long set of instructions.

For me, the simplest but most important routine is the one that occurs at the start of the lesson. How pupils enter the room, how they get ready for work, how the teacher greets them . . . all of these things set the tone. If this process is crisp, calm and clear, pupils will get an immediate sense of what kind of expectations the teacher has of them. If, on the other hand, things are sloppy, that is, there is no clear direction or leadership, and pupils are allowed to mill about and remain unfocused, the message will be somewhat different.

Reflection box:

What routines and expectations do you have of pupils at the start of your lessons? How frequently do you have to reinforce these, or do pupils automatically follow them? Are your routines the same for every class group, or have you had to adjust them according to the age, size and nature of the pupils?

Setting up a tight lesson beginning involves several considerations:

How do pupils enter the room? Ideally, it is a managed entrance: the teacher would be there first, greeting pupils at the door and fielding any problems as pupils enter (e.g. inappropriate uniform, excessive noisiness or excitement). Alternatively, pupils could line up outside the classroom and wait for the teacher to arrive, therefore giving the teacher a chance to establish calm and order in the line before they enter the room. The actual entrance could also be controlled, with pupils going through in pairs, or rows.

How are they encouraged to settle and focus? Having simple starter activities that pupils can get on with, without any explanation from the teacher, is a helpful way of engaging pupils whilst freeing you up to deal with other matters. Activities can range from the dry (copying the date, title, lesson objectives), to constructive (anagrams of topic-related key words), to fun (pictionary or riddles). A competitive element can generate added motivation.

How is equipment organised? Giving pupils clear expectations about where they can put their coats and bags, and what you expect to see on their desks (e.g. text books, stationery, *not* cans of drink or mobile phones) will help speed the process. For pupils who don't bring appropriate equipment, decide on a protocol – will you issue spares (that you collect in at the end), will they have to borrow from a friend, and/or will there be a small consequence? Give pupils responsibilities for giving out books and equipment, and try setting a time challenge ('A merit for everyone who can be ready by the time the alarm clock rings.').

How are latecomers dealt with? Inevitably there will be one or two students lagging behind the others, usually accompanied by some fantastical excuse. Establish a clear method for dealing with this problem: do not allow pupils to disrupt your flow or simply saunter to their seat. They should be expected to wait at the door (or even at a 'latecomer's table'), until you are able to deal with them, once the rest of the class is settled and on-task.

Any kind of routine needs to be practised in order for it to become the norm. For some class groups, particularly the more challenging ones, this may take longer. A behaviour support teacher explains:

I work all year on getting pupils to comply with the same set of expectations at the start of lessons: simple things like lining up quietly, or taking off their caps. It's frustrating that I am having to give the same reminders day in day out, and it takes time away from the main lesson, but ultimately I stick with it because following these expectations is an important lesson in itself.

If you are working with challenging groups (i.e. lots of problems occurring at once, difficulties getting whole-class control), focusing on a simple routine, such as what happens at the start of the lesson, can sometimes provide a 'way in'. Never mind stressing about what happens for the rest of the session (don't set yourself up for failure by expecting too much at once), if you can at least get pupils adhering to one or two straightforward routine expectations (e.g. entering the room in an orderly manner and immediately sitting at their desks), and give them the necessary support and praise, you are one step closer to reigning them in. I have been known to spend whole lessons working on how to line up at the door – it was tedious but worthwhile, because it established a basic standard. For particularly 'feral' classes you may want to recruit additional support, and there is no weakness in this. Even 'perfect' teachers can feel the pressure sometimes. A Head of Year comments:

I always make myself available . . . I have a hard, no nonsense reputation amongst the pupils. Staff will come to me if a class is being difficult, because my presence at the start of a lesson can help establish order and give them the breathing space to assert themselves. It's not about interfering or undermining their own skills to control their pupils; in fact, I think it gives a positive message about staff solidarity and teamwork.

Another useful tactic, when getting the whole class settled, is to focus your attention on the pupils who are doing the right thing. Instead of addressing the individuals that are not complying, which can feel quite negative, notice and give praise to those who are ready and waiting. I find that this approach tends to draw all but the very hardened into the fold – people want praise more than they want criticism. And if you can get the majority of the class on your side, dealing with the one or two obstinate ones becomes easier.

> **Reflection box:**
> Do you tend to focus on the positives or the negatives? Is it the
> carrot or the stick? Pay attention to yourself when settling your
> class at the start of the lesson. Do you motivate your pupils to
> do the right thing through praise and encouragement? Or do
> you try to push them into it through reprimand?

Routines are not only useful for establishing order at the start of
a lesson – there are number of situations in which they can be beneficial. Whenever there is possibility of increased movement within
the room, such as transition between activities, clearing away, or
exiting the classroom at the end, following a routine can help
maintain order.

When clearing away, especially if activities have involved lots of
equipment and/or mess, having a structured approach reduces the
risk of pupils getting carried away and using the time as an opportunity to muck around. It is helpful to factor this time into your
planning, as an Art and Design classroom technician comments:

> I think the pupils should definitely be encouraged to take
> responsibility for clearing away the materials they have used, but
> if this is rushed or they aren't encouraged to do it sensibly, things
> get damaged. Teachers need to make sure they have allowed
> enough time at the end for proper tidying up – it's just as impor-
> tant as the rest of the lesson. Pupils need to learn the value of
> things.

Here are some hints and suggestions for efficient and orderly
classroom organisation:

- Give work a home. Get pupils to place unfinished/finished
  work in separate trays. The finished tray can be checked by
  you, and work in the unfinished tray can be chased up later
  in the week.
- Provide a time limit. Encourage pupils to work productively,
  by setting a time challenge and reinforcing this by using an
  alarm.
- Play music, something motivating like the theme to 'Mission
  Impossible'.

- Avoid giving pupils an instruction that involves moving out of their seats (e.g. to tidy stuff away, or move to another area of the classroom) and then expecting them just to get in with it — maintain order, but staggering their movement, for example, allowing a table at a time to move.
- Assign responsibilities, either to individual pupils or to tables (e.g. 'pupils on the big table need to collect the work, pupils on the square table need to wash the paint palettes'). To make it fair, rotate responsibilities.
- Encourage independence. If pupils can be trusted to sharpen pencils at the bin, or collect stationery, without having to ask for permission, you will be harassed less frequently.
- Establish simple rules for problem areas, such as no more than two pupils using the sink at a time, which will ease congestion and reduce the chances of foolery.
- Set consequences for pupils who muck about or damage equipment — demonstrate that you take it seriously.
- Aim to allow some time after tidying-up, for pupils to sit back down and focus, before the lesson ends — creating a neat finish to the lesson.
- Manage the way in which pupils exit the room. Either table by table, or make it fun/reward focused: pupils whose names begin with 'P'/pupils who have earned a merit/pupils who have handed their homework in/pupils who are wearing blue . . .

A crisp, structured end to a lesson is just as important as a crisp start. The time can be used as a plenary, to reflect on pupil's efforts, to praise and reward, to set or collect homework, to quiz pupils on their knowledge, or to throw in a lighter pupil/teacher bonding moment — to have a joke or chat. If pupils leave on a lingering high, they will be looking forward to their next lesson with you. If they leave in an orderly manner, they will be heading to their next lesson or break, in a calm frame of mind.

Key points for setting up routines:
> The most effective routines are simple and easy to enforce.
> Use them at key points in your lessons: the start, the end, clearing away, and transitions (e.g. moving from one activity to another).

> Pay attention to how pupils enter the room. Wherever pos-
  sible, be there to establish good order before they come in,
  and manage their entrance, so that they don't all bundle in
  together.
> Use routines as a way of establishing basic standards of com-
  pliance with very difficult classes.
> Notice the pupils who are getting it right, rather than focus-
  ing on the ones who aren't.
> Encourage pupils to see the value of classroom property by
  taking the tidying-up process seriously.
> For messy practical activities, factor tidying-up time into
  your lesson plan – view it as an integral part of the lesson
  content.
> Motivate pupils to tidy up quickly, by playing music or
  setting a time challenge. Warn pupils who muck about that
  they will have to make up the time.
> Aim to end the lesson calmly, and release pupils in a control-
  led manner.

Time management and paperwork

Being in the classroom is only one aspect of a teacher's duties. Yes.
It's time to think paperwork. Not everyone's favourite word,
I realise, but one that we can't overlook. Some members of my
discussion group were particularly vocal when it came to this issue.
The obvious burden of increasing paperwork is the pressure it
places on a teacher's time. Time is not something that is generally
on the teacher's side anyhow. I have had very few – if any – conversations with teachers who feel they are able to get everything
done within the school day. Either they work through their evenings, weekends and holidays; or they resign themselves to the idea
that they will never be as efficient and organised as they'd like to
be. A teacher training lecturer comments:

We have to focus on what is realistic, what is achievable, and
then balance this with what is effective. We can't do it all, because
we simply don't have the time. And when it comes to weekends,
well, I'd rather see my teaching students have a life outside of

work . . . it's important to refresh yourself – sometimes it's more important than a file of perfect lesson evaluations.

A typical teaching day takes 5 or 6 hours, and within that, the teacher may be required to do a break/lunch duty, maybe to take pastoral responsibility for a tutor group, to lead extra-curricula activities, chase up pupils for homework/behaviour issues, and to attend a number of weekly meetings, which may last until five in the evening. This is before the planning and paperwork has even started. And what of the paperwork? This could include the following:

- Lesson plans (long term/medium and short term), schemes of work, worksheets and other teaching resources – differentiated as necessary!
- Lesson evaluations
- Timetables
- Pupil assessments, marking classwork, homework, coursework and exams, setting targets
- SEN forms, IEPs, annual reviews
- Pupil reports: subject, form group, department
- Pupil certificates
- Letters to parents, memos
- Risk assessments for trips and activities
- INSET applications and feedback
- Performance management, threshold forms
- Writing up incidents

Reflection box:
How do you manage your paperwork? Do you stay on top of it or do you just do what you can when you can? Do you find yourself worrying about the things you haven't done?

Unfortunately, I cannot wave a magic wand and remove all your paperwork pressures, but rest assured, I do believe there are ways of coping with them. Starting with that all-important realistic expectation of what you can achieve ('perfection' in the real world) – if you tire yourself out trying to do it all, you will not be at your best when it comes to the important bit: teaching your pupils. Other wisdoms came from different members of the discussion group. A deputy head explained:

> As senior management, I am inundated with demands on my time. When it comes to paperwork I have to be ruthless. Either I deal with it there and then, make a plan for when I will deal with it, pass it on to the person that should be dealing with it, or put it in the bin.

Allowing pieces of paper to pile up aimlessly creates mess, stress and a sense of impending doom! 'To do' trays are usually a bad idea as well – invariably they turn into a dumping ground that becomes less and less appealing as it grows. If you are receiving endless memos and forms and feeling like you haven't got time to complete them properly, just fill them in as you can. Invariably, people are looking for a quick response rather than a thorough, carefully considered one – if they want more information, they can always get back to you. Whenever I am requesting information from staff, I make sure that my memos are as user-friendly as possible, perhaps requiring nothing more than a tick in a box – this means I get them back quickly.

It is always worth questioning the value and purpose of the piece of paper in front of you. Is it important? Does it need a bit of extra care and attention? Is it urgent? Prioritise your workload, so that if you cannot get everything done, at least you can get the important things done. For routine paperwork requirements, such as planning and marking, try to establish a set time in the week for when you will concentrate on this. Make the most of any Planning and Preparation Time, and if you use it productively, you shouldn't need to feel guilty about not doing any work at home.

Reflection box:
How constructively do you use your non-contact time? Do you have access to everything you need? Do you have a quiet, distraction-free space to work in? Does it help to give your self time limits (e.g. 30 minutes marking, 30 minutes planning, 20 minutes general admin)?

I don't advocate taking paperwork home, unless the circumstances are exceptional. For the sake of your sanity, a clear difference between the work and home environment is vital. In the same token, don't overwork yourself in the school building either. A primary school teacher cautions:

> Recently my school has seen a trend of people getting in really early and then leaving as late as possible. It's as if everyone is competing to prove that they are working the hardest . . . I hope my head teacher confronts it, because it is creating an unhealthy atmosphere. Despite being more organised, people seem more stressed.

Which comes back to the idea of balance. For some teachers it is a matter of looking inwardly and questioning their own perception of their achievements. So many of us consider ourselves to be perfectionists, but does this do us any favours, when in reality, and in our minds, perfection is always one step away? So many things can go wrong in a school day (many of which are beyond our control), and sometimes our hard work seems like it is coming to nothing. From my own experience, I know that the times when I am striving to be really great at my job are also the most stressful. When I sit back a bit, and say I'll just be 'good enough', I relax – and I enjoy it an awful lot more.

Key points for time management and paperwork:

> - Learn to prioritise, and where possible, deal with things as soon as you get them.
> - Create dedicated time for routine tasks, such as planning and marking.
> - Give yourself time limits, and don't spend a long time agonising over tasks that simply don't merit it (i.e. half an hour writing a plan for an activity that lasts 10 minutes).
> - During busy times, for example, report writing, plan some easy lessons and cut back on marking.
> - Aim for a balance between what is realistic and what is necessary/helpful to you.
> - If necessary, adjust your own expectations of yourself – my idea of a 'perfect' teacher is a happy all-rounder, not a stressed out paperwork god/goddess.

Working with teaching assistants and other staff

Managing pupils is a tricky business, but when it comes to managing other staff, well that's something else entirely. Depending on the nature of your subject and/or your pupils', you may find that you have a number of different adults available to support you, throughout the day or for certain lessons. Teaching assistants, special needs assistants, mentors, advisors and classroom technicians. Given the daily pressure faced by the average teacher, any extra support should be a blessing, but, for an unfortunate few, it can also be a curse. A senior teacher explains his experience:

> Most of the TAs I've worked with have been great, but a handful have created more problems than they've solved. Either they've found it difficult to take direction, which causes friction, or they've needed too much direction. Some have been downright lazy. It's a burden to have to 'carry' problem staff, especially when the pupils are handful enough.

Reflection box:
Think of the relationships you have with your support staff. If they are successful, what makes them so? If they are problematic, why? What would need to change in order for things to improve?

The dynamics of the relationships between adults in the classroom can have an impact on a number of things, for example: mood and atmosphere, pupil behaviour, levels of stress, organisation of the room, organisation of lesson activities, and pupil motivation. In a sense, we are providing a model of how adults relate to one another – we are setting an example. Personally, I believe that pupils are very quick to pick up on this sort of thing, and will use it to their advantage.

So what does an effective teacher/assistant relationship look like, and how can the 'perfect' teacher achieve this? And what does a bad relationship look like? This can range from a quietly negative atmosphere to full-blown arguments. A dysfunctional relationship will inevitably lead to tense, unhappy pupils, high levels of poor behaviour, missed opportunities for positive action, bad organisation and stress.

In some environments, the teaching assistants are the backbone of the school. They may outnumber the qualified teachers and will have considerable responsibility — the line between teaching and assisting is become increasingly vague. Nonetheless, their salaries have been allowed to remain low. Are they being taken advantage of? One head teacher suggests:

> Teaching assistants could be fundamental to the future of education. They are not 'poor little things', and should be treated with respect, given necessary training opportunities, good hours, financial gains and job satisfaction.

An assistant's ability to be effective, and to make the best of her/his skills, can often be dependent on how effective the class teacher is in managing them. If the relationship between the two is not effective, we cannot always assume it is the fault of the assistant. In fact, an OFSTED inspector once jokingly quipped that if a teaching assistant folds her/his arms and looks bored: fail the lesson! But managing staff, as has been aforementioned, can present quite a challenge, even for experienced teachers, as explained by a secondary English teacher:

> I'm so used to being the only adult in my classroom, I find the thought of sharing it quite intimidating. I'm worried that they will judge me or compare me to the other teachers they work with. It's not that I mind telling my pupils what to do, but I don't have the confidence to do it to other adults.

Management of adults is a skill in itself. Some people are naturally assertive, and others are happier sitting back. Directing or giving orders to another grown-up, as opposed to a pupil, naturally poses more challenge because it feels more personal — we don't want to put the respect of our colleagues at stake. On the other hand, effective management has little to do with bossing people around. It is perfectly possible to lead a team and get on with them

at the same time. It simply requires confidence, fairness and a positive, can-do attitude. An experienced teaching assistant explains:

> The best kind of teacher to work for is the one that listens to
> your point of you, values your contribution (i.e. asks for your
> opinion), does the things they say they will, is clear about what
> they want from the pupils and is able to have a laugh with you
> at the end of the day. They don't have to be the most efficient
> teacher or the one that gets the best results . . . but there has to
> be some mutual respect there.

Perhaps increased training opportunities in how to build successful teams would be beneficial.

Key points for working with teaching assistants:

> - Focus on the ideas of solidarity and teamwork. Refer to the
>   things that 'we' do rather than what 'you' and 'I' do.
> - Value staff by asking for their suggestions and advice, and
>   making use of their ideas. Remember that they may know
>   more about the students they work closely with than you do.
> - Assign clear, specific responsibilities, and make use of indi-
>   vidual strengths (e.g. artistic skills, organisational skills, a
>   caring nature).
> - Whenever possible, involve staff in planning, and at the least,
>   take opportunities at the start of the lesson to talk through
>   your expectations of how they can get involved.
> - Show appreciation (the occasional doughnut is always wel-
>   come), offer encouragement and let people know what they
>   do well.
> - Turn differing personality 'styles' into strength (e.g. good
>   cop/bad cop) – contrast can work as long you still stick up
>   for the same principles.
> - Aim for common understanding of what you want to achieve
>   in the classroom – communication is vital.

5 School life beyond the classroom

Coping with stress

According to the headlines, millions of working days are lost each year due to stress-related illness. The teaching profession is often considered to be one of the worst culprits. It's not hard to work out why it is a potentially stressful career: along with a heavy workload and lots of responsibility, the classroom is an unpredictable place. Managing people, whether they are children, adolescents or other adults is very demanding, and if other issues are thrown into the mix (e.g. pupils with challenging behaviour or pupils with special educational needs), the demand becomes greater. Add to this the various different government initiatives that are, some say all too frequently, thrown at us; the pressures of inspections; league tables; action plans; targets; financial worries , the list goes on. But sometimes the origins of stress can be internal, as a secondary school teacher explains:

> I'm often my own worst enemy because I'm such a perfectionist
> . . . I want to do the best job I can, and if I don't think its good
> enough, I blame myself . . . I end up worrying that I'm not good
> enough. And when it comes to things like lesson observations
> and inspections, I have sleepless nights for weeks. Sometimes,
> the only way I can cope is by telling myself not to care so
> much.

Reflection box:
What makes you feel stress? What are your triggers? Make a list of all the things that bother you, either work related or personal. How frequently do you encounter these issues? Pay attention to your experiences throughout the week, giving yourself a mark out of ten for how stressed you feel in different circumstances.

It is worth remembering that stress can affect anyone, from trainee teachers to senior managers; and that the triggers of stress can vary from person to person. Amongst my discussion group, common factors included the following:

Fear of failure, particularly for those who are inexperienced.
Feeling as if you have 'forgotten' how to teach, which commonly occurs after a holiday or a weekend.
Fear of the unknown, when facing new classes, a new school or responsibility.
Fear of the known: anxiety about teaching difficult class groups or individual pupils.
Feeling unable to cope with the workload: too many tasks and not enough time.
Feeling unable to switch off: thoughts and concerns about teaching and pupils encroaching on your personal life, for example waking you up at 4 in the morning!

It is also important to understand that not all stress is problematic. At a certain level, it plays a vital role in motivating us to get things done; it spurs us forward and encourages us to make improvements and find solutions. Without it, the world would be a different kind of place. But stress becomes unhealthy, and potentially damaging, if it is excessive, unmanageable and relentless. A deputy head teacher made an interesting remark:

The fact is, we wouldn't have really amazing schools if we didn't have those people who give their all, and who put themselves on the line. This in itself isn't stress: it's passion. If teachers are suffering with stress, I think it's largely because of the expectations from above.

So what are the signs and symptoms that stress is going too far? Unfortunately, stress can be insidious. It can build up slowly and quietly, and isn't always recognised until 'breaking point' is reached. A helpful way to avoid reaching breaking point is, first, to be aware of your own stress triggers (see reflection box above) and, second, to recognise the symptoms of stress. These may include the following:

General feelings of increased anxiety or worry (not just school related)

Loss/increased appetite

Disrupted sleep

Stomach upsets

Frequent illness (stress impairs the immune system)

Excessive tiredness and feelings of exhaustion

Feeling 'emotional' (tearful, short-tempered, aggressive, etc.)

Physical symptoms (weight loss/gain, hair loss, skin problems, twitches, headaches, nausea, jaw tension)

Feelings of panic or hysteria

Increased alcohol/smoking

Intense feelings of dread about going to work

Negative self-image and feelings of failure

Inability to wind-down and relax, even at weekends

Reflection box:

How does stress affect you? Talk to friends, family and colleagues. Do they notice any changes in you that you aren't aware of?

So what can be done about it? Whether you are just beginning to feel the pressure or you have already hit rock bottom, taking a practical approach will help. It all starts with recognising that you *are* stressed, that there is nothing wrong with being stressed (in the sense that it doesn't make you an inadequate or weak person), and reflecting on what is causing your stress.

You may encounter a few sceptics, the 'pull-yourself-together' brigade, but for every one of these, there will a handful of people who are able to empathise and relate to your experiences. It is perhaps a case of surrounding yourself with the people that are going to be most supportive.

If your stress-load is not too high, there are steps you can take to get it in hand yourself:

- Step back from the heat: give yourself some recovery time. Delivering a few 'easy' lessons, leaving early, and not doing any marking, isn't going to destroy the world. What's the worst that can happen?

- Set clear workload boundaries for yourself, for example. take your breaks, set time limits for paperwork tasks, only take one task home each night, delegate work to other people (assistants, sensible students).
- Establish systems that will make your general work life easier. This can be as simple as reorganising your files or tidying a cupboard, or more complicated: rearranging a timetable, or adapting the curriculum.
- Tell yourself that you will cope, and accept that you may not be able to do everything – but nor can anyone else.

If your stress-load feels overwhelming, it is important that you seek support from others. Sometimes having a rant, is the most effective way of off-loading your worries, and staff-rooms tend to be full of willing ears – we are all in the same boat. Sometimes it is a relief just to know that you are not alone. Shared humour also helps to diffuse tensions and creates feelings of solidarity. It may be necessary to express your issues in a more formal way. A trusted senior colleague, your GP, your union, and occupational health services should be able to advise and support you.

It's not just what happens in school that counts, but what happens out of it. Finding a work/life balance is a challenge that everyone faces, but it may well hold the key to a successful, happy and fulfilling existence. Teaching is often considered to be more than just a job – it is a vocation, a lifestyle choice. The 'perfect' teacher conjures up images of a devotee, someone who throws every bit of themselves into the role, but one member of my discussion group had this to say:

To be the perfect teacher you've got to have a bit of outside experience. You can devote yourself to your classroom, but ultimately, if that's all you do, it will be limiting. If you have a rich, varied life, you have different things to bring to the role.

Key points for coping with stress:
- ➤ Recognise that teaching can be a stressful job. Feeling stressed is not a sign of failure or weakness.
- ➤ Get to know your own anxieties about teaching, and recognise your stress triggers.

> Monitor your expectations of yourself: are they fair and reasonable, or are you demanding too much?
> Set clear boundaries for yourself, and recognise that you can't do everything – this doesn't mean that you've failed; it just means you are human.
> Learn to prioritise and delegate your workload – trying to do everything yourself is unrealistic and unnecessary.
> Seek support, either informally or formally.
> Make the most of your personal time – the consensus is that having a life outside of school will enhance your teaching, rather than hinder it.

Communicating with parents

The amount of contact a teacher has with the parents/carers of their pupils will vary according to the age group they teach, the ethos of the school, and ultimately, the willingness of the parent/carer to engage themselves. Primary school teachers may have almost daily contact with family members, as they come to collect their offspring from the school gates or classroom. As pupils get older, the connection tends to fade – the occasional phone-call or letter, or a 5-minute slot at parent's evening. And alas, there are always a number of parents/carers who seem to drop off the radar altogether, especially when they are most needed. A behaviour support teacher remarks:

> The parent of one of my most difficult pupils makes it impossible for us to contact her. She has several different phones that are never answered, and are switched off if she recognises the school number. I understand that she doesn't like hearing bad news about her son's behaviour, but I think she's neglecting her responsibility as a parent. And it means that the school always wastes time chasing around after her.

The twin environments of home and school are both pivotal in a young person's development; success and positive experiences in one will help individuals to succeed in the other. It would be great to think that every child experiences a continuum of care and encouragement and support, with parents and schools both upholding positive expectations of conduct and attitude, shared values, and mutual understanding of one another's roles and responsibilities. Unfortunately the reality can often be different. A further education lecturer highlights the struggle:

> I find it increasingly difficult to get parents in. We only ever seem to get the one's of the kids who are nice – the ones who really need the support never show up. If you ask me, it's the tip of the iceberg, if we're talking about underachievement in education. It's no good having a go at teachers . . . if the parents aren't interested, the kids aren't going to be.

Reflection box:
How much contact do you have with your pupil's parents/ carers? Does it vary from pupil to pupil? Does the amount of contact affect your relationship with the pupils?

Members of my discussion group felt strongly that issues going on in the home, and wider society, are reflected in what happens in schools. We hear a lot in the media about the changing nature of the family unit (extended families, single parents, teenage parents, high-divorce rates, etc.), and the breakdown of respect and social values. Inevitably then, this will emerge in schools.

It is not always a neglect of interest that is the problem. It can also be over-interest – the proverbial 'pushy' parent – or indeed, it can be, as one retired head teacher describes, the wrong kind of interest:

> I got fed up of parents coming in and asking us what they could do to help their child make progress at home. I'd say, take them to town, go to museums, go to the theatre, go for walks, do things, talk to them . . . but they didn't want any of that – they just wanted pages of sums.

So what can the 'perfect' teacher do to build positive links with parents/carers? Effective communication starts with openness. First of all it is a matter of being clear about when you can be contacted and how. This will depend on your individual circumstances, but it may break the ice if you send out a friendly note at the start of the year/term, introducing yourself and outlining your school contact details (not your personal contact details of course!). Making this welcoming first move helps to open up lines of communication that may not otherwise begin — some parents will be suspicious or wary of the school environment, and may not have the confidence to otherwise engage. As teachers, we can forget how scary it is to talk to our kind! Here are some other suggestions for effective communication with parents:

- Be approachable, smile and avoid an overly formal manner.
- Avoid using teaching jargon. Explain things clearly, and if necessary, prepare the key points you want to make in advance.
- Be diplomatic and express regret if talking about bad behaviour ('I'm sorry to tell you that . . .'). Be honest, but remain objective.
- Stick to the facts, and where possible, use concrete evidence to support what you are saying (registers, incident reports, class-work, marking sheets, etc.)
- If a pupil is going through difficult times, suggest frequent contact via email or a home/school book, so that progress can be monitored.
- For problem parents (those that are overly pushy, unpleasant or threatening) ask for additional support. Don't try to tackle them on your own.

One of the individuals in my discussion group expressed concern that the teaching profession has lost the trust of parents. As both a parent and a head teacher he warned:

We complained to our child's school because he wasn't being taught how to read adequately, but our concern wasn't taken seriously by the class teacher, so we wrote a four-page letter to the head . . . fortunately the issue was investigated and satisfactorily dealt with. The advice I give to my own staff is: if you are going to talk to parents, then treat them like adults and don't ever try to fob them off.

Key points for communicating with parents:

> Clarify how parents can contact you (e.g. by appointment, email, after school, a phone-call, a home-school book) – invitation may encourage more wary parents, and lay down boundaries for the demanding ones.

> Recognise that some parents may have an ingrained anxiety or mistrust of schools – you may have to tread carefully to build up trust.

> A special effort can make a big difference. Some parents will really value the support and advice you can give them – their support and sharing of information will, in turn, make your job easier.

> At parent's evening, use records and evidence as the basis for your discussion. Give parents the opportunity to ask questions, and make a note of their concerns.

> Seek support from other colleagues when dealing with challenging or aggressive parents.

> Never give out you personal/home contact details.

Relationships with teaching colleagues

This book began with the idea that teaching can be quite a solitary profession. We spend much of our day alone in our classrooms with our pupils, and contact with other colleagues/other adults is often limited. Nevertheless, a sense of staff camaraderie and teamwork is essential to an effective school. It matters for a number of reasons:

Communication: if information is effectively disseminated and shared, confusion and uncertainty will be reduced.

Consistency: common staff expectations and values provide a clear message to pupils and strengthen school policies.

Stress-relief: other staff can play a major role in offering support and perspective, given that they, of all people, will understand what the stresses are.

On the subject of communication, the discussion group had several valuable thoughts. The art of good communication is not just about what is said, but *how* it is said: the tone in which the message is delivered. Several people raised the issue of sometimes feeling patronised or talked down to:

I switch off during the head's speeches. He talks to us like we are school children. He tells us how to do our jobs, but in actual fact he doesn't have a clue – he never goes into classrooms and he hasn't taught since the 70s. I'm amazed he hasn't picked up on the fact that everyone sits there yawning throughout his meetings, but then again, he's completely lost in his own little fantasy world!

Others had more positive experiences. Several comments were made about the value of establishing 'systems' of communication, ensuring that messages reach the people they need to, and important information is passed on. For example:

A staff-room suggestion box, so that complaints and ideas can be written and posted anonymously.

A central notice board for sharing important non-sensitive information about pupils (e.g. arguments, rivalries, difficulties).

A clear protocol for getting assistance during an emergency (e.g. a fight or major disruption).

Senior staff having mobile phones/an on-call rota, so that there is always someone available.

Staff frequently checking their pigeonholes (simple, but effective!).

Regular staff meetings that are concise and have a focused agenda.

Information being disseminated via email, therefore reducing the paper trail.

Communication also needs to be seen as a two-way process. Both teachers and support staff talked of the importance of feeling involved in decision-making. Many said, that even if the decision was out of their hands, the chance to have their say really mattered. People like to feel that their point of view is valued and that it will be listened to. This sentiment is echoed in the experience of pupils and parents. A parent commented:

Some teachers see me coming down the corridor and think, 'oh god, it's her again', but I don't go into the school to make trouble. I go in because I care. If they give me the answers I need to hear, I leave them to get on with it, but I won't put up with less – my child's education is at stake.

A sense of 'openness' is helpful – an atmosphere in which everybody feels able to voice their concerns, successes and suggestions. If this is not encouraged, teams can quickly splinter, giving rise to gossip, backbiting, bitching and resentment. Perhaps a 'perfect' teacher is one that endeavours to facilitate this. From my own experience, I have found that some staff teams develop the skill of 'open' communication quite naturally, and others need more coaxing. I use weekly team-meetings as a chance to raise issues amongst the group, and also invite staff to approach me one-to-one if necessary. A head teacher for London echoes this approach:

> I see my role as a supportive one. I know that, at times, my staff will be knocked for six, so its important that they feel that I know what is going on around the school and that I am there to help – I make sure my presence is evident in the corridors, and the playground. And perhaps it's a cliché but 'my door is always open'.

A healthy staff team can make all the difference. In such a stressful and potentially isolating job, knowing that you can wander into the staff-room, grab a cup of coffee, and then laugh off your troubles or have a moan with like-minded colleagues is a good release. Some members of my discussion group even cited positive relationships with staff as a reason for staying in otherwise challenging schools.

Unfortunately sometimes it is the other colleagues that are the source of work place stress. Power struggles, personality clashes, conflicts and bullying: these are not uncommon amongst teams of staff. What is visible on the surface: the glossy school prospectus, the mission statement and the staff handbook, isn't always a reflection of the hidden workings of an organisation and the actual experience of staff and pupils. When the two sides align themselves, things become more comfortable, but if not, and if steps aren't taken to help them to align (e.g. senior staff understanding and taking measures to address the real-life, day-to-day struggles of the school rather than focusing on administration and policy), resentment sets in.

Individual staff can do their bit to create a supportive, open climate for one another. The 'perfect' teacher should understand their role not just in terms of what they do for their pupils, but what they contribute to the staff team. What this contribution is may depend on the individual. Perhaps you are the friendly, approachable joker. Maybe you are the patient listener and shoulder to cry on. Maybe your organisational and interpersonal skills mark you out as a natural leader. A good team recognises and makes the most of different qualities, but there also has to be some unity: a common purpose and an agreed sense of how to achieve it.

Reflection box:

How much time do you spend with colleagues? Do you visit your staff-room regularly? Do you attend social outings with other staff? Do you greet colleagues in the corridor?

So what does the 'perfect' teacher need to do in order to support colleagues? Perhaps it's easy to focus on what they shouldn't do:

- If you borrow other people's ideas, don't try to pass them of as your own. Give them credit.
- Share resources and make sure they are accessible to others who need them, that is don't hoard them in your own cupboard without telling anyone.
- If you borrow resources from other classrooms, make sure you remember to put them back.
- If a colleague is complaining about a difficult pupil or class, avoid using the phrase: 'they're never a problem for me'.
- By all means share ideas and offer advice, but be wary of sounding like a 'know-it-all'.
- Don't be afraid to ask others for advice or support – no one is invincible and admitting this encourages openness.
- But be wary of becoming the resident moaner. Try to think of something positive to say about your day when you meet with colleagues.

Key points for relationships with teaching colleagues:
> Effective communication is vital and in large schools, this may require a systemised approach.

> Healthy teams have an 'open' approach to communication – staff need to feel comfortable about raising concerns and challenging leadership decisions.
> Communication is a two-way process: listening is as important as talking.
> Camaraderie with other staff can make a difficult day seem bearable: don't cut yourself off from the staff-room.
> Know your own strengths and consider how you can make use of these within your team.

Extra responsibilities

After a long day of classroom teaching, sometimes the last thing on your mind will be running a busy activity club, organising a theatre production or sports event, or even just turning up for one of those many staff meetings. However, beyond the daily routine of delivering lessons, school life can offer rich opportunities for getting involved. Whether you are a budding artist, wannabe sports coach, or a closet union activist, there are bound to be possibilities to explore these interests, and do something positive for the pupils and the school as a result.

Members of my discussion group were enthusiastic about the benefits of engaging with wider school life, although time was often cited as a defining factor. A newly qualified teacher comments:

Because of my musical interests I've been asked to help out with school productions and band competitions. I'd really love to do it, but I can't afford the time, due to enormous amounts of paperwork. Plus I have my own family to look after. I hope that next year I'll be able to get more involved, because it looks like a lot of fun.

Getting involved in extra-curricular activities will inevitably require you to give up your own free time, so think twice before making a commitment, especially if you are relatively new to teaching, and should be focusing your energies on developing your teaching skills. That said, there is a lot to be gained from taking part in the realms of wider school life, and indeed, in some schools there may be an expectation that you do. Benefits include the following:

- Pupils seeing you in another light
- Seeing the pupils in another light
- Getting to know different pupils and staff across the school
- Getting involved in an activity that you enjoy (but may not necessarily teach)
- Developing new skills and experiences
- Adding to your CV
- Enhancing your 'reputation' around school
- Personal satisfaction

For some staff, the extra-curricular aspect of their career makes everything else seem worthwhile. A London teacher comments:

I quite enjoyed my job anyway, but it transformed when I agreed to organise a charity fun-day. We did lots of silly activities across the school, and it was a big success, although it was a lot of stress and extra work. After doing it, I felt like people treated me differently – the pupils had this newfound respect for me, and senior management seemed to notice me more. The benefits definitely outweighed the negatives.

Reflection box:
What can you offer to your school? And what can your school offer you? Do you have hidden talents that you could share or a burning ambition to give something new a try?

Another teacher, now retired, comments:

The extra things we used to organise, like staff pantomimes and themed days – at the time we always used to moan and get annoyed about the time and effort involved, but ultimately, they generated some great memories and were always a good laugh. Going that extra mile gives you a sense of occasion and camaraderie.

Another valuable aspect of school life is the trips. For pupils and staff alike, getting away from the four walls of a classroom, whether for a week or just a day, can provide the most memorable experiences of all. It may also give pupils opportunities that would otherwise be inaccessible to them. An inner city primary school teacher explains:

> When I took a class to visit a farm last year, I was amazed that most of them had never seen a cow or a pig before – their only experience had been through the TV . . . I grew up in the countryside, so their excited reaction was quite a shock to me. It gave me a different insight into their lives.

Running a trip is, of course, a big responsibility, and has to be carefully planned and risk assessed. If you intend to organise one, but haven't had previous experience, these are the things you will need to consider:

- School policy: make sure you are aware of legal obligations, and have completed any necessary risk assessments/health and safety forms. Ask for guidance if you are not sure.
- Pupil supervision: do you have enough staff to run the trip? Can you get parents involved?
- Get your administration organised: letters home, reply slips, raising and collecting funds, booking venues and transport . . . there are lots of things to sort out, so where possible, plan in advance.

But it isn't all just fun fun fun. There are many other aspects of wider school life that teachers are required to be involved with, such as meetings, and duties, and depending on your role, managerial tasks, curriculum responsibilities, and the delivery of INSET. All of these things are essential to the smooth running of a school, but not always liked:

> Sometimes it feels like I'm jumping from one meeting to another. And some of them just go on and on. I wouldn't mind if we were talking about useful stuff, but it tends to get lost

beneath the rambling – some people like the sound of their own voice too much.

A purposeful, focused meeting can be a valuable way of pulling ideas and information together, but if it isn't carefully managed, the above can happen. And there is nothing more frustrating than sitting through an over-long, aimless discussion, when you know that there are a million other things you need to get done.

Reflection box:
Think of a typical meeting in your school/department. What sort of things make them unproductive (e.g. too many people, too long, lack of clear purpose)? What makes them productive (e.g. someone driving it forward, time limited)?

So how does the 'perfect' teacher take control of the meetings that they attend and run? Here are some tips:

Length: after a days teaching, useful contributions will be hard to maintain for anything more than an hour. Thirty minutes is even better.

Clear purpose: many schools have to organise the cycle of meetings well in advance, but there should be flexibility to make changes as the year progresses. Meetings shouldn't take place for the sake of holding them, as this will destroy the patience and goodwill of the staff.

Focused agenda: items should be considered in order of priority so that important things don't get rushed through at the end. The agenda should be issued in advance, and success often lies in specifying and restricting the purpose of the meeting, so that it doesn't turn into a free-for-all rant about everything that's wrong with education.

Someone chairing: although meetings are often run by the most senior staff members, this should be a facilitating role and not an authoritative one. Turns could be taken, encouraging more collaboration between staff at different levels and reducing the stigma of 'power'. The chair should maintain focus by drawing a line under off-task discussion and summarising key points.

Key points for extra responsibilities:
> Getting involved with clubs and activities can enhance your work life, and enable you to see another side of your pupils.
> Beware of the time-commitment, however, and don't take on more than you can cope with.
> If you feel under pressure, ease off, and don't be afraid to say no to things.
> Trips can provide meaningful opportunities for staff and pupils alike, so don't be afraid of them, but ensure you a following the required school policy and are well organised.
> Aim for meetings that are brief, focused and purposeful.

Observations

Like them or loath them, classroom observations are a part of school life. And it's not just NQTs that have to put up with them – observations continue throughout a teachers career, whether they are part of an inspection, peer observations, or routine monitoring by senior management. At best, they can provide a positive critical framework for evaluating your practice, honing your skills, and developing your strengths. At worst, they can pile on the stress and dent your confidence. An experienced secondary school teacher laments:

I know I can teach, but the idea of having my practice scrutinised always makes me anxious. I never perform as well during observation lessons as I do in general, because my nerves get in the way. It used to infuriate me because I knew I wasn't showing off my true capabilities, but now I just reassure myself that I know my own worth, and that other people's opinions don't really matter. Ironically, since I've started thinking like that, I've definitely felt less nervous.

And on the other side of the coin, a head teacher comments:

I'm really not trying to catch anyone out, but there is sometimes a perception that lesson observations are unfair or cruel things. For me, it's about making sure – as some one with overall responsibility for the school – that I know what goes on in our classrooms and that a standard is being met. If teachers have got nothing to hide, then there should be no need to worry. And I'm always aware that what I observe in one lesson may not be representative of that teacher's overall abilities.

Reflection box:

How did your last lesson observation go? Was the feedback what you wanted it to be? Did you feel it was a fair reflection of the lesson itself, and of your teaching in general? What effect did the feedback have on your confidence levels?

So how would the 'perfect' teacher display their abilities at their most perfect? I asked the discussion group what helped them to perform well during observations and suggestions included:

Be prepared. It is worth going that extra mile with plans and resources if it gives you an added sense of effective organisation.

Do something you can trust in. A number of teachers admitted that they drew upon or even repeated activities that had been previously successful, in order to showcase their abilities.

Prime the observer. Before the lesson begins it can be helpful to highlight any significant issues, such as the context of the lesson, location of pupils with SEN, pupils with behavioural difficulties.

Don't be put off by disruptive pupils. If problems occur, follow the accepted school protocol for dealing with them. Remember that you are not being judged on how they behave (that is up to them), but on how you manage their behaviour.

Remember to keep the ending tight. Keep an eye on the pace of the whole lesson, and allow time for a proper plenary, where pupils can share and demonstrate what they have learned.

After an observation you should be given feedback on your performance, either in written or verbal form. Hopefully this will be delivered thoughtfully, and will leave you feeling invigorated and confident. But if things don't go as well as you'd hoped, there may be the possibility of a second chance. A primary school teacher explains:

> I was observed during one of those total disaster lessons, where everything that could go wrong did go wrong, and I felt really dreadful about it. Fortunately my mentor was sympathetic, and said she would rip up the observation sheet and give me another chance. And this time, the lesson went smoothly. This sort of supportive approach is important, because we all have our bad days, and we shouldn't be judged on the basis of them.

The result of any lesson observation should be to improve the quality of teaching and learning, but this won't happen if teachers have their confidence knocked by the experience. Feedback should be positive and encouraging, as well as constructive; and if not, there should be room to challenge judgements that seems unfair.

Key points for Observations:
> - Like it or not, they are an on-going part of teaching culture, and staff at every level of experience has to go through them.
> - Good preparation will help you to feel confident in yourself and therefore increase the chances of you having success.
> - If it helps, do an activity that you can trust in, but don't be afraid to use it as an opportunity to show off how fabulous you are.
> - Feedback should be constructive – if you feel that an evaluation or comment was unfair ask for advice from a supportive senior colleague.

Final thoughts

Perfection. Perhaps everyone has her/his own personal idea of what this means and represents to her/him. For some, it is having tight organisation and immaculately presented files of paperwork. For others, it might involve inspired, off-the-wall lesson ideas that grab pupil attention. And for others still, it may be about making meaningful social breakthroughs with tough and disengaged youths.

But ultimately, the quest for perfection of any type is a difficult one. Writing this book has highlighted to me, and hopefully to you as readers, that the issues and challenges within daily school life are diverse and unpredictable. We can learn to cope and to work with these challenges, but we also have to have a realistic perception of what effect they can have on our achievements. It's hard to be perfect when the rest of the world isn't.

So the next time you find yourself feeling a bit defeated by difficult pupil behaviour, or staring anxiously at the hefty pile of lesson plans belonging to the smug teacher sitting next to you, remind yourself that perfection doesn't count in the long run. What truly matters, on a day-to-day basis, is that teaching is a career that feels exciting, manageable, worthwhile, and, at times, extraordinarily wonderful.

Index